A Layperson's Guide to Biblical Interpretation

A Means to Know the Personal God

Luke Brad Bobo

Foreword by
Clarence Dewitt Agan III

RESOURCE *Publications* • Eugene, Oregon

A LAYPERSON'S GUIDE TO BIBLICAL INTERPRETATION
A Means to Know the Personal God

Resource Publications
An Imprint of Wipf and Stock Publishers
199 W. 8th Ave., Suite 3
Eugene, OR 97401

www.wipfandstock.com

PAPERBACK ISBN: 978-1-4982-0889-5
HARDCOVER ISBN: 978-1-4982-0891-8

Manufactured in the U.S.A.

This book is dedicated to Rita (wife), Briana (daughter), Caleb (son) and my 'Superman' and beloved grandpa, the late Henry S. Bobo (July 3, 1922 – May 2, 2011)

" . . . there is no God like you in heaven above or on earth beneath, keeping covenant and showing steadfast love to your servants who walk before you with all their heart."

—1 Kings 8:23

Contents

Figures and Tables

Foreword

"MAN DOES NOT LIVE by bread alone, but by every word that proceeds from the mouth of God" (Matthew 4:4, ESV). When Jesus utters this sentence—a direct quotation from the Old Testament (Deuteronomy 8:3)—he affirms two foundational truths: God speaks, and he speaks clearly enough that human beings can derive life-giving sustenance from all of his words. But if God has spoken, and he has spoken in words that real people can understand, then we, as the recipients of God's words, have to consider a pressing question: what must we do to *rightly* understand what God has said? What interpretive approaches will help us chew, swallow, and digest these words that are given to satisfy our deepest spiritual hunger? The book before you is intended to help you answer this question, which is why I am so happy to recommend not only that you read it, but that you practice what it teaches.

My friend Luke Bobo is an experienced educator and Christian leader with a passion for helping real people wrestle with profound questions. If you are searching for practical tools to help you understand the Bible better, Luke will be a faithful guide. If you are looking for principles that will help you understand what distinguishes careful interpretation of God's words from careless *mis*interpretation, you will find helpful instruction here as well. And I am convinced that this book will be of benefit to you even if you are still not sure whether God has spoken, or whether we are capable of grasping what he says in the Scriptures. Tasting the sweetness of the bread can go a long way toward convincing us that the baker is wiser and more loving than anyone else who has ever fed us!

Luke and I first met almost 20 years ago, when he was a student in my Greek classes at Covenant Theological Seminary in St. Louis. There I observed in him one of the characteristics that qualifies him to write this book: before he is a teacher of the Bible, he is first and foremost a student of the Bible. Luke is able to help others as they wrestle with interpreting Scripture because he himself is an experienced wrestler. Learning Greek isn't always easy, but if it would help him understand God's words, Luke was going to wrestle that language, and all its complexities, all the way down to the ground! That leads me to a second observation. Luke is that rare breed of person who has excelled in the arena of formal theological training, yet who has remained passionate about teaching others who have had no such training. Often a person with such passion will neglect his own seminary studies; and often the gifted seminarian will teach "over the heads" of real people. Luke has done neither. His commitment is to helping every person know God and understand God's word to the best of their ability, regardless of spiritual pedigree or educational background. Given that God seems to have made me equal parts pastor and scholar, I find in Luke a kindred spirit.

But what about the subject matter of *Layperson's Guide to Biblical Interpretation*? Why is it so important? My experience as a pastor and teacher of pastors suggests three key reasons to me. First, this book recognizes that if God has spoken, then God has the right to determine what his words mean. This may sound counterintuitive; after all, if only God has the right to say what the Bible means, then why should we bother learning how to interpret the Bible? Here, though, is the crucial point that my friend Luke grasps so clearly: biblical interpretation is not a futile endeavor leading to a dead end where we find out that every person has the right to choose the meaning that best suits them. Instead, properly understood, biblical interpretation is the activity by which human beings discover what God meant by the words he spoke. God's words, like all words, were originally spoken in a complex web of intersecting contexts. As we learn more about those contexts, we come closer and closer to understanding what God originally intended. For example, if I say, "Hit it again," you aren't sure what I mean. But if you know that I am a musician shouting to my bandmates onstage during a concert, you could infer that I mean, "Let's play that song one more time." Alternatively, if you know that I am a mechanic, and you see my partner holding a hammer as we try to loosen a stubborn bolt in the garage, you reach a different conclusion: I mean, "Hit the bolt one more time, because it's not loose yet." Or, if I'm a character in a spy movie, and I speak those words to a woman who has just said, "The canary flies by day," you realize that my words are part of a secret code that means, "I am the agent you were sent to meet; it's safe to talk." Similarly, when God originally spoke the words of Scripture, he spoke them into a contextual web with which the first hearers/readers were familiar; by speaking into that context, God asserted his right to determine what his words meant. Our task is to follow the threads of this contextual web until that meaning becomes clear. Sometimes this task is simple, and sometimes it is challenging—but it is never a dead end.

Second, *Layperson's Guide to Biblical Interpretation* exhibits an intellectual integrity forged in real relationships. When it comes to interpreting the Bible, a teacher needs to "know his (or her) stuff." But if that "stuff" is communicated in ways that are abstract, jargon-filled, or concerned with insignificant details, it only reinforces the idea that a true understanding of the Bible is reserved for the members of some elite inner circle. That leaves people feeling that they have three options: join the inner circle, and begin talking about God's word as though it never intersects ordinary life; pretend to be in the inner circle, just to impress those who are; or give up on the possibility of really understanding what God has spoken. By contrast, the best teaching about the Bible and its interpretation will never force such options on us. Instead, it will marry profound, intellectually rigorous insights with the kind of speech God has given us in his word—speech that is meant to be understood by real people, in the circumstances of real life. Put simply, because he knows and loves real people, my friend Luke understands that the way we talk about interpreting the Bible sends signals about the Bible itself. If we are careless and intellectually sloppy, we send the signal that the Bible is insignificant, not worthy of serious thought; but if we sound elitist, we are teaching that the Bible isn't meant to be understood, because God wants only a small group to know him well. Because Luke doesn't believe these things about God's word, he marries real-world clarity with intellectual depth.

Third, this *Layperson's Guide* continually demonstrates that a right understanding of God's words requires a combination of right skills plus right attitudes. Students of Scripture often gravitate toward one of these extremes. Some people assume that "if my heart is right," then my conclusions about what God is saying in his word will always be correct—or, if not correct, at least safely protected behind an attitude of sincere piety. If love for Jesus is my chief guide in interpreting Scripture, then for you to question my interpretive conclusions is to question the sincerity of that love— the height of rudeness! Others come from the opposite approach: if I have applied the right methods, the right skills, the right procedures, then the interpretation I have arrived at will be correct, even if my heart remained cold, hard, and unmoved during the process. As you read this book, you will be steered away from these extremes. You will learn new skills and ways to evaluate your understanding of Scripture. At times, you will be told that a favorite interpretation is incorrect, or that a familiar interpretive method is unhelpful—and it may hurt your heart to hear it. But you will also be challenged to engage your heart more fully, to approach God with humility and gratitude, to trust the power of God's Spirit, and to grow in your love for God's Son. Skill and attitude will be interwoven, with each shaping the other. You will learn how to recognize that when Jesus speaks of "bread" in Matthew 4:4, it is a symbol for food in general; and that when he refers to "the mouth of God," he is employing a figure of speech rather than indicating that God the Father has a human body. But you will also learn that our interpretive efforts have failed if our hearts are not moved to see our need of God's life-giving words! God has spoken, and he has spoken in ways that real people can understand. And when we have *rightly* understood his words, we will love him more deeply. May you experience this reality as you learn from an author who is mature in both understanding and love.

C.D. "Jimmy" Agan III

Senior Pastor, Intown Community Church
Atlanta, GA

Preface

THIS BOOK IS NOT for everyone; this book was written specifically for *one* audience. This book is for the layperson; the person with *no* seminary training. This book is for the faithful Sunday School or Bible Study teacher. This book is for the Christian who wants to take a "deeper dive" into Bible Study. This book is for the Christian person who wants his head and heart challenged and transformed.

So, let me contradict what I wrote earlier, this book is for everyone—even the seminarian who wants to be re-acquainted with the basics of Biblical interpretation.

Acknowledgements

WRITING IS EXHILARATING, ON one hand, and quite challenging, on the other hand. Writing this book was not without its challenges. However, those challenges were greatly mitigated because of the support of many dear people. That brings me to offering thanks to a host of friends. Many thanks to the BBT Staff for allowing me to take a two-week sabbatical from writing curriculum to give my undivided attention to this book. Thanks to a quartet of superb writers in their own right: Rita Holmes-Bobo (my wife), Briana A. Bobo (my daughter), Dr. Charlene Engleking ('twice a doctor') and Lisa Mann, BBT colleague, for reading and offering feedback on what had to be an unattractive and unwieldy draft.

Thanks to the fine students of the Spring 2014 Christian Ministry Studies (CMS) 3010010 Hermeneutics Class – one of my last classes taught at Lindenwood University (St. Charles, MO) - Jordan "Rosa Parks" Mueller, Mary Purnell, Chase Stewart, Malach "Mal, Mal" Radigan, Emily "Word Queen" Bounds, Katelyn "Kat" Marsh, Xiaodong "East Brother" Shi, Mikaela Lauren Carr, Jacob Divich, William "Billy" Farr, Kristen "Biscuit" Graham, Connor Johnson, Wesley Kuhn, Samantha McCord, Andy Sengsavang, Samuel "Sam I Am" Vermeer and Elizabeth "Lizzy" Wasiuta - because unbeknownst to them I was teasing out the contents of this book, stealthily, during this course.

And thanks to those Faith Ascent Base Camp *Track 201* cream of the crop high school students who enrolled in my very, very short course on *Hermeneutics,* where the contents of this book first made their debut. Unbeknownst to them, they were my 'guinea pigs' in which the acronym of *SCAR* (Sit, Context, Analysis, and

xvii

Redemptive Remedy) was tried. Feedback and questions from this bright group lead to some additional refinements of *SCAR,* and thus, this layperson's guide to biblical interpretation.

Finally, I would like to acknowledge those who have trained me in this field of hermeneutics either in class and/or through their writing: Drs. Clarence DeWitt "Jimmy" Agan, III, Dan Doriani, D. A. Carson, Robert Smith, Jr. and Richard A. Young.

I would like to extend a special acknowledgement to Dr. Jimmy Agan because he labored reading through an early draft of this book and he wrote the Foreword to this book. However, there is one more reason why Dr. Agan deserves a special acknowledgement: his devotions before class and his infectious love for Greek are so memorable these many years later after graduating from Covenant Theological Seminary that I have remained one of his biggest fans.

Introduction

"If doctrine is presented with joy and accuracy, the hearers
will not only stand it, they will crave more of it."[1]

—Robert Smith, *Doctrine that Dances*

WHAT (OR WHO) MAKES you grit your teeth and grunt, "argh!" out
loud? Doctrine presented inaccurately annoys me. Moreover, mis-
interpretations and thus, misapplications of God's Word exasper-
ate me. Here are four instances that make me grunt, argh!

- Instance #1: I once heard a speaker say this, "God wants us to
be rich [materially] because Jesus became poor that we might
become rich." This speaker based this bold but outrageous and
absurd statement on 2 Corinthians 8:9, "For you know the
grace of our Lord Jesus Christ, that though He was rich, yet for
your sake He became poor, so that you through His poverty
might become rich." What are the interpretive mistakes? The
first interpretive mistake is a failure to understand the wider
literary context which begins in 2 Corinthians 8 where Paul
commends the Macedonians' generosity in giving despite
them facing persecution and despite these saints being in dire
financial straits. The second mistake is reading a foreign meaning into the words "rich" and "poor." Here Jesus 'became poor'
by taking on human flesh and living as a servant (see Philip-
pians 2:6–8) so that we might 'become rich'—being granted
salvation with all the associated benefits. For this speaker to

1. Smith, *Doctrine that Dances*, 6.

1

conclude that God wants us to be rich materially is foreign to this text and foreign to the rest of Scripture.

- Instance #2: A TV minister, who will go nameless, encouraged his tuned-in TV listeners and parishioners in the pews to write personal vision statements based on Habakkuk 2:2b, "Write the vision." In fact, he went on to give an example of a personal vision statement by saying, "Make it a goal to be married in 10 years." Comments like this beg the question: what happens if this goal is not met? The interpretive mistake here is failing to consider the meaning of the word "vision" and the larger literary context of Habakkuk 2:2-20. Recorded in Habakkuk 2:1, the prophet awaits God's response to his rebuke. Verses 2-3 is the Lord's response. The Lord commands Habakkuk to "write the vision." In other words, Habakkuk was told to write God's revelation ("the vision") on tables of stone so that mankind might read it quite easily. This text does not support the writing of a personal vision statement; rather, the prophet Habakkuk was encouraged to write God's message for perpetuity and to encourage His people.

- Instance #3: A Christian student, I formerly taught at Lindenwood University (St. Charles, MO), adamantly and unwaveringly declared that getting tattoos was forbidden based on Leviticus 19:28, "You shall not make any cuts in your body for the dead nor make any tattoo marks on yourselves: I am the Lord." A discussion of the interpretive mistakes are to follow.

- Instance #4: I have heard Christian parents tell their kids, "don't hang out with unbelievers" because "bad company corrupts good morals." These parents justifiably and confidently base this prohibition on 1 Corinthians 15:33. A disclosure of the interpretive mistakes are to follow.

In all four instances, there was a total breakdown in rightly interpreting the text and, thus, rightly applying the text. The interpretative mistakes have been briefly discussed for the first and second instances. Let's explore the interpretative mistakes of instances #3 (Leviticus 19:28) and #4 (1 Corinthians 15:33) at a deeper level.

To Tattoo or Not Tattoo:
That is the Question[2]

The first place to begin when interpreting Scripture is to ask, what is its purpose? In this case, what is the purpose for Leviticus? *Answer*: the book of Leviticus gave the *young* Israelites a prescription for holy living. The Israelites were young in terms of being new in their relationship with Yahweh; thus, He leaves nothing to chance but rather lays out what He considers to be holy living. Leviticus 19:28 is a good example of what holy living looks like for the Israelites and by implication, us, as well.

We find these words recorded in Leviticus 19:28 (NIV), "Do not cut your bodies for the dead or put tattoo marks on yourselves. I am the Lord."

At first blush, it appears my former student is quite correct in stating that Christians should not desecrate their bodies with tattoos. This appears to be an 'open and shut case.' But wait—in order to rightly interpret this text, we need to ask a few exploratory questions first. For example, here are some questions and answers.

1. *What is this book of the Bible chiefly about?* The book of Leviticus is about how unholy people are to practice holiness before a holy God. For example, the book of Leviticus prescribes, in excruciating detail, how one approaches and appeases a Holy God in worship. But living holy includes our day-to-day interactions with foreigners, unbelievers and believers, and the treatment or stewardship of our bodies, as in Leviticus 19:28. All areas of life—home life, community life, civic life, and work life—provide ample opportunities to worship, because obedience honors God.

2. *This verse is surrounded by other verses, what do they tell us?* Leviticus 19:3-36 gives God's people (the Israelites then, and us today) specific details on how to live holy.

---

2. I strongly encourage the interested reader to consult Travis Scott's fine article, *Decorating or Desecrating the Temple?* on Ransom Fellowship's website, ransomfellowship.org.

3. *Where were the Israelites—had they entered the Promised Land yet?* The Israelites are still in the wilderness, but on the cusp of entering the Promised Land. So, here God instructs His people what holy living looks like among people who are not holy. In this passage, God prohibits His people from participating in pagan mourning rites by cutting their bodies for the dead.[3]

Notice what this passage forbids: getting a tattoo that illustrated one's allegiance to a pagan god, and thereby volitional participation in a pagan mourning rite. So what can we conclude? This passage does not forbid a Christian from getting a tattoo, because many tattoos today do not have the same pagan associations as they did for the Israelites at this time in history. This is not to say that getting a tattoo or other marks on the body should be a mindless decision; rather, Christians must engage their minds and carefully weigh the pros and cons of getting a tattoo. In other words, while we are free to get tattoos on our bodies, it might not be the wise or God-honoring thing to do.

Keeping Company with Unbelievers: Yes or No?

What do we make of 1 Corinthians 15:33? Does this passage justify that believers, in Jesus Christ, should not keep company with unbelievers?

As in the previous example, our initial question is about the context of 1 Corinthians 15. Paul is discussing the centrality of the bodily resurrection of Jesus, for the foundation of our faith and for our future bodily resurrection. In short, without Jesus' resurrection, we are essentially existentialists[4] living by this motto, "let us eat and drink, for tomorrow we die" (see vs. 32b). After carefully examining the historical context of this Scripture, we realize that many influential Corinthians considered the bodily resurrection

---

3. Sklar, 250.

4. This worldview teaches that "life is absurd." Since there is no underlying meaning or creator, we create our own meaning.

4

of Jesus to be inconceivable. The church at Corinth was a spiritually, doctrinally, and theologically troubled church.

Upon closer examination of 1 Corinthians 15:33, we see that Paul is actually quoting a line from a lost comedic play of Menander entitled *Thais*. By quoting this line, "bad company corrupts good morals," Paul recognizes that some Christians in Corinth were denying the bodily resurrection because they had adopted an alternative eschatology.[5] They were spending time dining in the temples with those who espoused a viewpoint of eschatology that lined up with Roman Emperor. Roman Emperors, like Augustus, not only wanted residents to adopt them as the fulfillment of a divine plan and of prophecy but they also wanted residents to focus on the past and the present and *not* the future.

"The 'bad company' points to those who were teaching that there is no resurrection and so were a threat to the testimony of the church."[6] The Apostle Paul therefore, in verse 34, urges the Corinthians to stop sinning in denying the resurrection of the dead and, by implication, the resurrection of Jesus Christ—because this led to hedonistic lifestyle especially among the rich and educated. Based on this analysis, should Christian parents use this passage as a means to justify that their kids not associate with unbelievers? An emphatic, "No!" I had a seminary professor who often said this, "Don't hear what I am not saying." That is, while this passage cannot be used to justify not associating with unbelievers, if an unbeliever is leading you to undermine the testimony of the church by denying a foundational doctrine, then you should think twice about associating with this unbeliever!

This Book

This book is simply about how to rightly interpret the Bible. If we *rightly interpret* the Bible, then we can *rightly apply* the Bible, and *rightly live* by the words of the Bible. Notice the order: rightly

5. The study of end times or future events.
6. Mare and Harris, *1 & 2 Corinthians*, 116.

interpret, rightly apply, and then rightly live. Suffice it to say, there is much at stake for the Bible interpreter; this is especially true in a time where bad Biblical teaching and preaching not only goes unchallenged, but unfortunately is being paraded as good Biblical teaching and preaching.

Consider my two 'juvenile' process flow diagrams:

1. Wrong interpretation → wrong doctrine → wrong application → wrong living

2. Right interpretation → right doctrine[7] → right application → right living[8]

Biblical interpretation has an end-game. It affects how we live now! If we start with a wrong interpretation, the end game is wrong living or living that does not line up with God's Word. Legalism and moralism, the two ugly twins—are often birthed and resurrected as a result of wrong interpretations. Legalism has the appearance of holiness, but actually coaxes our vulnerable sinful nature to do unholy things. Legalism says "follow these man made rules as a sign of living holy." Moralism says "be good" or "be like King David, slay your Goliaths." Both legalism and moralism give the 'what' without giving us the 'why'. However, if we do our due diligence to arrive at the right interpretation (with the aid of the Holy Spirit, of course), we are able to live rightly, in concert with God's Word, and as we live rightly, we will truly honor God in all that we say and do.

Biblical Hermeneutics Defined

The technical phrase for Biblical interpretation is Biblical hermeneutics—where hermeneutics is the *art* and *science* of interpretation. But why "science," and why "art"? This may seem counterintuitive because the words "science" and "art" trigger different parts of our brain. How can Biblical interpretation be both *an art* and *a science*?

---

7. Formal or technical name for right doctrine is *orthodoxy*.
8. Formal or technical name for right practice or living is *orthopraxis*.

Why "science"?

As a former electrical engineer for more than fifteen years and a lover of mathematics and science, the word *science* brings these words to my mind: precise, *accuracy,* and exactness (again, refer to Dr. Smith's quote at the beginning of this chapter). We must endeavor to be *exact* in our interpretation of God's words. Consider D. A. Carson's passionate appeal, "We are dealing with God's thoughts: [so] we are obligated to take the greatest pains to understand them truly [accurately] and to explain them clearly."[9]

Notice the order: we must understand God's thoughts first, *before* we can explain them clearly. Otherwise, we might be tempted to share our thoughts and not God's thoughts.

Why "art"?

You may not remember Hiram of Tyre. 1 Kings 7:14 not only describes him as a "worker in bronze," but "he was full of wisdom, understanding and skill for making any work in bronze." Hiram was a skilled artisan; he knew which tools to reach for to make the pomegranates (7:18), the sea of cast metal (vs. 23) and the ten basins of bronze (vs. 38). Likewise, there are several "tools" at our disposal as Biblical interpreters to confidently and correctly interpret God's Word. I will introduce these hermeneutical tools later, so stayed tuned. Our task is to become 'skilled artisans' by choosing the right tools when doing Biblical hermeneutics. Being a 'skilled artisan' takes practice . . . practice . . . practice. In short, we must become *exacting artisans* when interpreting God's words by pulling from our 'hermeneutical toolbox' the right tool (or set of tools) that complements the interpretative task at hand.

Terminology

A word about terminology is in order. Among those who interpret the Bible, you will often hear the words exegesis and eisegesis. Here are two overlapping definitions of exegesis that I favor. First, "the

9. Carson, *Exegetical Fallacies*, 15.

term exegesis . . . is a fancy way of referring to interpretation. It implies that the explanation of the text has involved careful, detailed analysis."[10] And second, "Exegesis refers to the careful, rigorous, exacting, meticulous and thorough interpretation (hermeneutics) of a literary work. Interpretation is the act of explaining the meaning of something."[11]

By exegesis, we then mean exacting the true and right meaning *out* of the text. *Eis*-egesis is the opposite. Eisegesis is the reading of *another meaning into* the text that is foreign to the author's original intent. We want to avoid, eisegesis, or 'reading into the text,' and pursue relentlessly, exegesis, 'exacting out of the text.' (Note to the reader: I will use exegesis and Biblical interpretation interchangeably.)

The Subject of Our Inquiry Is the *Holy Bible*: *So What is the Bible?*

The Bible is God's full disclosure, or revelation, of His thoughts. As we read it, it is apparent that God condescends to communicate in a language accessible to us. God uses words like "Father," "rock," "sand," "birds," "fortress," "hand," "head," "shepherd," "foot," "body" . . . and many more words like these to make His word and most importantly, Himself, accessible to us. As such the Bible is a means of grace, where *our Holy and Transcendent God bows to communicate with us.*

Additionally, the Bible is a unified, coherent redemptive-historical story or "theo-drama"[12] given in four[13] major acts:

- Act 1: *Creation*—captured in Genesis 1-2; this scene pictures God as a thoughtful worker creating a "shared habitat"[14] for in-

---

10. Kaiser and Silva, *Biblical Hermeneutics*, 19.

11. Young, *New Testament Greek*, 1.

12. Kevin J. Vanhoozer refers to the narrative of Scripture as the 'theo-drama' in *Whatever Happened to Truth*, Andreas J. Kostenberger (Editor).

13. Some say there are five acts to this redemptive story: creation, treason/rebellion, redemption, church age, and consummation/restoration.

14. I first heard Dr. Cal DeWitt, Professor Emeritus, University of

sects, animals, and mankind. This time in history is marked by bliss. This time in history also marks the perfect communion between God, and genitors of the human race, Adam and Eve.

- Act 2: *Treason/Rebellion*—by eating of the forbidden fruit, Adam and Eve broke fellowship with God, transgressed His covenant and committed treason against Him. As a result of this one act of treason, sin has intruded God's world and the damaging effects of sin continue until this day. And because of our first parents' misstep, all mankind is capable of doing some extraordinary beautiful things *and* additionally, all mankind is capable of doing some extraordinary baneful things too.

- Act 3: *Redemption*—redemption reached its climax with the birth, death, burial, resurrection and ascension of Jesus Christ. However, there were 'sign posts' along the way in the Old Testament that intimated this event.

- Act 4: *Consummation/Restoration*—at the end of history Christ will restore all things. Creation will be restored, our human bodies will be restored, and our relationship with God will be fully restored. All, who confessed faith in Christ, will live in perfect bliss with God and His people in the new heavens and the new earth.

I strongly encourage you—*if you have not done so already*—to read the Bible cover-to-cover to get the "feel" of this magnificent story. If you like, set this book aside for a moment, read this beautiful story on the pages of the Bible, and return to this book!

The Bible captures *one* theme: God's gracious dealings with His people and His world, which reaches its climax through the work and person of Jesus Christ, the "seed of Eve."[15] So then, the Bible compiles a rich redemptive history with God as the main and primary protagonist. This redemptive history, while distant from us, can be lived out; in this way, this history provides us principles to live by that are *gnomic* (always true at all times). Lastly, the Bible is not

Wisconsin Nelson Institute for Environmental Studies, use this phrase.

15. This author believes Jesus' supreme climatic work was His bodily resurrection from the dead.

a science book; rather, the Bible is literature and is written by many human authors—inspired and steered by the Holy Spirit—who employed a wide assortment of genres, literary devices, and idioms unique to their culture and times. However, you will soon discover that the same literary devices that these biblical authors used are still in use today such as: metaphors, similes, hyperbole, and repetition.

A Word about Bible Translations

There are a plethora of Bible translations on the market, but please note that "not all translations are created equal." Michael Dundit[16] has written a fine piece on the differences between the translations presently on the market. (So excellent that it has been reprinted here almost verbatim below.) In this article, Dundit explains how all Bibles fall into one of three categories: formal equivalence, dynamic equivalence, and paraphrases.

Three categories

There are three major categories that represent different approaches to expressing the biblical revelation (originally recorded in Hebrew and Greek) into English.

1. Formal Equivalence

A Formal Equivalence translation takes a word-for-word approach—that is, for each Hebrew or Greek word in the biblical text, the translators have sought an equivalent English word that will communicate the same idea.

The beloved King James Version (KJV) is such a translation, as is the Revised Standard Version (RSV).

In more recent years, the New American Standard Bible (NASB) has become a popular study Bible because of its very literal rendering of the original languages. But because of the emphasis

16. See http://m.lifeway.com/Article/so-many-choices-what-makes-one -different-from-another.

on word-for-word accuracy, the NASB (which is at an 11th grade reading level) doesn't read as smoothly as many other translations. That makes it a great study Bible, but not ideal for public or devotional reading.

A recent Bible translation that has grown quickly in popularity is the English Standard Version (ESV), first published in 2001. The ESV seeks to combine word-for-word accuracy with literary beauty and readability. It also retains many classic theological terms that some other modern translations avoid.

2. Dynamic Equivalence

Unlike the word-for-word translation philosophy of the first group, this category seeks to take a middle road between a literal translation and a thought-for-thought approach to translating the biblical text.

That is, rather than trying to find an equivalent word or words for each word in the original biblical text, the translators have tried to stay close to the literal meaning of the words while also seeking to capture the ideas of the biblical authors with equivalent language to capture those thoughts in the English text.

The best known Bible in this category is the New International Version (NIV), which for many years has been the top-selling translation among evangelicals. The NIV is a very readable translation (aimed at a 7th grade reading level). This translation approach means that there are points where the English text reflects an interpretation of the biblical text, rather than a literal [translation]. For example, where the biblical text may specify a specific cost (100 denarii), the NIV might substitute the value in other terms (four months of a worker's wages) to make the cost more understandable for the reader.

The Holman Christian Standard Bible (HCSB) is a bit of a hybrid version, in that it uses a translation philosophy called "Optimal Equivalence." That means the HCSB switches between word-for-word and thought-for-thought [translations] depending on the translation team's views on a particular passage. The HCSB is also an original translation from Greek and Hebrew texts, as contrasted with those that grew out of KJV tradition, such as RSV.

3. Paraphrases

A paraphrase is a very free rendering of the biblical text in thought-for-thought approach.

In other words, the paraphrase is less concerned with translating the actual words of the text than with capturing the ideas of the biblical author and expressing those [ideas] for the unenlightened Bible shopper going into a *LifeWay Christian Store* to select a Bible, it is a bit like going to a Walmart superstore to pick a box of cereal—with the huge selection, where do you even start?

The first well-known paraphrase for many evangelicals was The *Living Bible* (LB), in which Kenneth Taylor took an English translation and rephrased it into modern American speech so that anyone (even a child) could understand the message. The *New Living Translation* was developed by a team of scholars and published as a revision of the LB to enhance the accuracy of the text while retaining the readability of the paraphrase. The most popular paraphrase of recent years is *The Message* by Eugene Peterson. It uses contemporary American idioms to keep the language of Scripture fresh and understandable. While not designed for serious study, it's a common choice for devotional reading.[17]

Dr. Luke's Advice

Use a formal equivalent translation when doing your Biblical interpretation. Consult the dynamic equivalent translations and paraphrases to bring clarity to the formal equivalent translation, or use them as resources. I suggest this order because in many cases the paraphrases and dynamic equivalent translations are the fruit of another person's Biblical interpretation. In other words, if you reach for a paraphrase or dynamic equivalent too early, this can 'rob' you of the hard (and rewarding and fun) work of doing

---

17. Technically, many scholars would say that a paraphrase begins and ends with the same language, as with the *Living Bible* (LB): English original (KJV) yields English paraphrase (LB). On this view, the NLT and *The Message* are translations, since the translators did begin with Greek/Hebrew.

Biblical interpretation on your own. For example, consider Psalm 23:5b from the English Standard Version (a formal equivalent) and the Living Bible (a dynamic equivalent), respectively:

ESV: "You anoint my head with oil."

LB: "You have welcomed me as your guest."

Research tells us this: before and after Jesus' incarnation, to anoint a house guest's head with olive oil would be equivalent to regarding this person as a special guest. This is exactly Jesus' complaint with Simon in Luke 7:46. Compared to the sinful woman's action of anointing Jesus' feet with ointment, Simon's hospitality was woefully lacking because he did not anoint Jesus' head with oil. Jesus was not treated as a special guest. If you skip over doing the research and reach immediately for the LB translation, you will be 'robbed' of the opportunity to discover this on your own.

Expectations

There are five expectations an exegete (or Biblical interpreter) must know at the outset, before actually doing Biblical interpretation.

First, expect to apply your research skills to this task. Each time you embark upon the task of Biblical interpretation, you are embarking upon a mini-research project. Yet, this research will pay handsome dividends, such as you falling more and more in love with Christ, Our Lord and Savior!

Second, expect some hard and arduous work. The author, Veith, sums up well why we can expect hard work, "The revelation of an *infinite* God by its nature must be complex, multifaceted and challenging to the human mind."[18] Our minds are fallen and finite and we are handling the thoughts and words of an *infinite God*!

Three, expect to know God more deeply. James I. Packer tells us why, "God's purpose in revelation is to make friends with us."[19] Imagine that—God wants to make friends with us! And God has

18. Veith, *Why God's Word*, 36.
19. Packer, *God Has Spoken*, 50.

chosen to reveal Himself by two accessible means: in Creation[20] and by His Word. So, expect your relationship with God to go to a different, sweeter, and more personal level.

Fourth, expect that your sense of discernment for good exegesis will become sharper as you listen to sermons and hear (or participate in) Bible Study lessons. "Victoria" would attest to this. I taught Victoria at an apologetics summer camp. She has since asked me several questions, and none as satisfying as this: "I went to a different church, and the pastor was speaking about the afterlife; and much of it I had not heard before (after many years of teaching) and it made me uneasy. Could you listen to it and let me know what you think?" Like Victoria, as we study and interpret the Bible on our own, our "uneasy antenna" will become more and more acute to detect bad interpretations, and thus unsound doctrine or teaching.

Finally, expect those you teach to crave your teaching more and more. Refer back to Smith's quote at the very beginning of this chapter. He writes, "If doctrine is presented with joy and accuracy, the hearers will not only stand it, they will crave more of it."

Book Layout

This book is comprised of two parts. Part 1 includes Chapters 1–5. Part 2 contains Chapters 6–7. Specifically, in Chapter 1, I provide you some general principles that govern the Biblical interpretative task. I refer to these principles as 'hermeneutical principles' or HPs. After a discussion of these HPs in Chapter 1, I then explain a four step process for rightly interpreting God's Word using this acronym: SCAR[21]—where S means to "Sit" with the passage

---

20. See Psalm 19 and Romans 1:18–32.

21. I used this acronym for the first time during the Faith Ascent Base Camp (Summer 2014) at Lindenwood University (St. Charles, MO). When I mentioned the name "SCAR," a student in the front row remembered Scar from the film, *Lion King*. Nevertheless, check out Faith Ascent—a ministry devoted to teaching high school students apologetics before they enter often hostile-to-gospel college environments.

of Scripture (Chapter 2); *C* is the *Context*—Literary and Cultural-Historical—(Chapter 3); *A* is *Analysis* (Chapter 4) and finally, *R* is *Redemptive Remedy* (Chapter 5).

Following a discussion of each letter of "SCAR" in Part 1, in Part 2—"Pulling it All Together," I will apply "SCAR" to two Old Testament passages in Chapter 6 and to two New Testament passages in Chapter 7.

Happy interpreting, fellow exegete!

Part 1

Hermeneutical Principles and Introduction to *SCAR*

1

Hermeneutical Principles

"Discipline is the bridge between goals and accomplishment."

—Jim Rohn

ONE OF MY GREATEST vocational joys was my time spent at the Francis Schaeffer Institute (FSI) at Covenant Theological Seminary in St. Louis from August 1999 to June 2007; there I proudly served as FSI's Director. The mission then, and still today, is "to train God's servants to demonstrate compassionately and defend reasonably the claims of Christ upon the whole of life."

One way we lived out our mission was through a popular event known as "Friday Nights at the Institute" (or FN@I) where Christians were invited to speak on cultural artifacts from a Christian perspective . . . with one caveat—they had to avoid using a lot of Christian language. One such talk was given by a dear brother, Mark Robinson, on the topic of jazz improvisation. The title of his talk was "John Coltrane: Contingency and Constraint."

It can be summarized this way: "jazz improvisation is both contingency (freedom to create) and constraint (bounded by basic rules)."[1] I like how he juxtaposed freedom with boundaries. As we seek to rightly interpret Biblical texts, however, eisegesis is not allowed—or we do not have the *freedom* to create meaning as we desire—as we are *bound* by a set of rules or principles.

1. Facebook message from Mark Robinson, May 18, 2015.

In this chapter, I provide some basic rules for doing Biblical interpretation. Here are ten (10) practical hermeneutic principles (HP) that anyone can use. In some cases, I have provided a specific *discipline* to exercise.

HP#1. The Holy Spirit is our chief superintendent when doing biblical interpretation.

Think of the Holy Spirit like the AV-8B Harrier[2]—a military aircraft that not only vertically lifts off, but, but *hovers* too. We must invite the Holy Spirit to "hover" over us as we begin on the interpretive journey, because, "the recognition of revelation *as* revelation must itself be the work of God—more accurately, the work of the Spirit."[3] It is only the Holy Spirit who can truly illuminate the Holy Scriptures and "confirm the truth that [God] has revealed"[4] to us.

Discipline: Ask the Holy Spirit to hover over you or help you as you interpret as only He, as God, can rightly discern the thoughts of God (1 Corinthians 2:10–16).

HP#2. *Context is Emperor!*[5]

Passages in the Bible must be interpreted *in their rich context*. Most of the interpretative process occurs here, as we must consider two important contexts:[6]

2. Prior to teaching, I worked full time as an engineer and part of my tenure as an engineer was spent working for McDonnell Douglas (now Boeing) in St. Louis, MO. One of the perks of working for a military aircraft manufacturer was seeing the planes that we produced. One such plane was the vertical take-off and hovering aircraft known as the Harrier.

3. McGrath, *Theology*, 135.

4. Adams, *Truth Applied*, 143.

5. Or "Context is King" or "Context is Monarchy." The former statement I heard repeatedly from Dr. Jimmy Agan and the second has been quoted by Dr. Jay Sklar. Both Agan and Sklar were professors of mine at Covenant Theological Seminary, St. Louis, MO.

6. There is a third context that I have termed the "Redemptive-Historical Context." This context is interested in where the passage falls along the redemptive-historical timeline. During this stage, we look for progress, continuity, development, or other patterns through the periods of redemption. This

- *Literary Context*—here, you must ask how do the verses around your passage and, the book in which the passage of Scripture (POS) is placed, aid you in understanding your passage;

- *Cultural-Historical Context*—here, you must ask about rituals, customs, social conventions, dress, architecture, family structure, and climate. You must also ask: what was happening politically, religiously, militarily, environmentally, economically and philosophically, etc. at that time.

If you fail to consider both contexts, you risk misapplying God's Word; and you effectively risk misquoting and misrepresenting God! Although more will be said about these two important contexts in Chapter 3, let's consider some brief examples of each context and how each one clarifies the meaning of a passage of Scripture.

Literary Context Clarifies Meaning

Consider the word "mystery" in Colossians 1:26–27. This word is not so mysterious after all because if we consider the *literary context*—namely, all the verses around it—Colossians 1:24-2:5, we find that "mystery" is God's unfolding redemptive plan through the finished work and person of Christ. Eugene Peterson's *The Message* Bible confirms this meaning of "mystery,"

"This *mystery* has been kept in the dark for a long time, but now it's out in the open. God wanted *everyone*, not just Jews, to know this rich and glorious secret inside and out, regardless of their background, regardless of their religious standing. The *mystery* in a nutshell is just this: Christ is in you, so therefore you can look forward to sharing in God's glory. It's that simple. That is the substance of our Message" (Colossians 1:26–27).

Knowing the literary context prevents us from reading our definition of mystery into this passage of Scripture.

particular context is not discussed in this book.

Cultural-Historical Context Clarifies Meaning

Why did Judah regard his daughter-in-law, Tamar, as a prostitute in Genesis 38:12–15? Judah assumed Tamar was a prostitute because of her lone presence by the roadside. So, the cultural-historical context answers our question: Tamar's lone presence by a roadside conveyed to her clueless father-in-law, Judah, that she was a prostitute (see also Jeremiah 3:2 which ties "by the road" with prostitution).

Consider Luke 10:4 also. On the surface, Jesus' instruction to His disciples to "greet no one on the road" seems rude and rather, unChrist-like. However, authors Klinck and Kiehl provide this helpful insight, "at times people overdo even friendly greetings and hospitality, and the Oriental custom tends to become long, drawn out, and repetitious."[7] So, instead of wasting time in meeting these customary social obligations, Jesus wanted His disciples to proclaim the gospel. Without this insight, we would think that Christ was training his disciples to be socially rude to strangers.

HP#3. Beware of the influence of your "traditions."

When we interpret Scripture, we bring many assumptions to the table based on our own life and history. These assumptions are influenced by our gender, our experiences (the good, the bad, the ugly), our ethnicity, our denominational affiliations, and our traditions. While there is nothing inherently wrong with our stories, we must be very careful not to allow ourselves to see the Scriptures solely through these personal lenses. I agree with the author, Carson, when he writes, "it is all too easy to read *traditional interpretations* we have received from others into the text of Scripture."[8] We must always allow our passage of Scripture to speak louder than our own assumptions, and louder than what others have told us (including mom and dad, our denominations, our systematic theology and what we have always heard about a passage). I remember a student who grew up in a certain denominational tradition; and

---

7. Klinck and Kiehl, *Everyday Life*, 164–65.

8. Carson, *Exegetical Fallacies*, 17.

his tradition taught that one can lose his or her salvation based on John 15:1–9. And he stood adamantly firm on his denomination's conviction; that is, until he took my course on Biblical interpretation. He discovered that this teaching was incorrect.

Discipline: Ask God to help you read passages as though you were reading them for the first time. And ask God to attenuate the other voices.

HP#4. Honor the original meaning of the text.

We *are not to* ask, "What does this passage of Scripture mean to *me*," as this is known as the "reader-response"[9] method. This particular interpretation method is bad news as it is open to anyone's guess, personal preference, and experience. The reader-response method of interpretation is like interpretation by committee, and is not recommended. Instead of asking what this passage of Scripture means *to me*, we must ask "what did *God intend* for this passage of Scripture to mean?" In other words, while a passage of Scripture may have many applications, a passage of Scripture, a verse, chapter, and a book can *never* mean what it was not intended to mean! Or, as one elderly Christian brother put it, "a verse [a book, a chapter] has *one* truth but many applications. To illustrate this point, consider Table 1 below.

9. See Kaiser and Silva, *Biblical Hermeneutics*, 33.

Table 1. *One* Original Meaning and *Many* Applications

Passage of Scripture	What is the Original Meaning?	Applications
Psalm 1	This wisdom psalm is about two ways to live, and two corresponding outcomes	Acquiring wisdom does not happen by osmosis; rather, we must read and meditate on God's word. Happiness is not found in the lifestyle of the ungodly. We should pray for those who follow the ungodly way as we know their fate.
Esther (entire book)	The entire book of Esther is about God intervening, and turning the tables in favor of His people	God is often inconspicuously acting behind the scenes to turn our awful situations—experiencing unfairness on the job—into fair situations. Our deliverance sometimes occurs at the intersection of God's sovereignty and our human responsibility.

Passage of Scripture	What is the Original Meaning?	Applications
Luke 18:1-8	This passage is about being persistent in prayer	All those who are 'destitute' should be persistent in prayer. Those who pray demonstrate their faith in God. Those who pray demonstrate "living by faith and not by sight" (2 Corinthians 5:7).
John 13:1-20	This passage is a picture of what humble servant leadership looks like; and where foot-washing serves as an illustration of humility.[10]	Rendering humble service means nothing is beneath my dignity to do—like changing the bed pan of an elderly person who has loss control of his bowels.[11] Biblical leadership demands serving those who follow you. Husbands lead their families by serving their family.

Discipline: Avoid the 'reader-response' method of interpretation. Do the necessary hard work to discover God's original

10. Some denominations have taken the application of this passage a bit further and made 'foot washing' a church ordinance. That's not the intent of this passage.

11. My late mother-in-law, Shirley A. Holmes, did this type of work in a

intent of the passage as the Bereans did! (Residents of the city of Berea in Acts 17, the Bereans were considered of more noble character than the residents of the city of Thessalonica). We can commend the Bereans for two reasons:

1. The Bereans did not take what the highly credentialed Apostle Paul was saying for granted; and;

2. They *examined the Scriptures* themselves (see Acts 17:11). The word 'examine' means to "sift up and down, *make careful* and *exact research* as in legal processes in the Scriptures for themselves."[12] I pray that you model this noble attitude of these Jews of the Berean synagogue.

HP#5. Every word is divinely inspired in the Holy Bible; however, the paragraph and chapter breaks are not divinely inspired.

This means that we should not rely on chapter breaks or paragraph breaks to determine the limits of our passage of Scripture (more about determining the limits of our passage of Scripture later). Chapter or paragraph breaks were not in the original Hebrew and Greek texts, they were simply added by English translators for our reading convenience.

Beginning in Genesis, for example, Genesis 1 ends at verse 31 in our English Bibles; however, Moses' train of thought does not end at verse 31; rather, it continues to and concludes at Genesis 2:3. So, Genesis 1:1-2:3 captures his singular stream of thought. In like manner, the narrative of David's thrilling victory over the taunting and sacrilegious Goliath runs 1 Samuel 17:1 through 18:5. In the book of Ephesians, the gospel imperatives are meant to impact one's home and social life; thus Paul applies the gospel to the family unit and society in Ephesians 5:22 through 6:4 (or 6:9).

---

nursing home. She was a beautiful example of a servant.

12. Robertson, *Word Pictures*, 314.

HP#6. Being familiar with the Bible can actually be an enemy of understanding the Bible.[13]

We have either said or heard any combination of the following before: "I know this passage of Scripture by heart" or "I know this Biblical story" or "I have heard this passage of Scripture preached or taught before." And while all of these statements might be true, I also agree with the author and my colleague, McCullough, who reminds us that "reading or absorbing the Word of God requires an open mindedness, an attitude that you haven't heard it all before."[14]

Discipline: Pray and ask God to allow you to see and hear the passage of Scripture as though you were seeing and hearing it for the very first time.

HP#7. The interpreter must exercise exegesis (seek the intended meaning) while diligently guarding against eisegesis (reading in a personal interpretation).

Exegesis occurs when the interpreter *draws out* the intended meaning from the passage of Scripture and *eisegesis* occurs when the interpreter reads his/her interpretation *into* the passage of Scripture. Sadly, there are too many examples of the latter in our culture. For instance, the prosperity gospel, radical feminist theology, and liberation theology are three incorrect outcomes of many Bible interpreters practicing eisegesis instead of exegesis. All of these incorrect outcomes began with an initial foreign framework. For example, those with prosperity gospel leanings come to the Bible with this belief about God: God wants me to be materially prosperous, so this belief is imposed on passages like 2 Corinthians 8:9. Similarly, radical feminist theologians approach the Bible this way: God is a God for the oppressed. Women have been oppressed by men; so God seeks to level the playing field. Thus, radical feminists read the Bible through the lens of this belief system. So, passages like 1 Timothy 2:8–15 are seen as not relevant to our time and

13. Dr. Robert Smith, Guest Lecturer for the Covenant Theological Seminary J. R. Wilson Preaching Lectures, Fall 2005.

14. McCullough, *Sense and Spirituality*, 48.

are dismissed. Liberation theologians, like radical feminist theologians, see God as a liberator from the oppressor. So, instead of seeking the intended meaning of the text, liberation theologians impose a liberation motif on passages that were never intended with this meaning.

> HP#8. Scripture interprets Scripture. African theologians dubbed this practice the "analogy of faith."[15]

In other words, we "reason by analogy from clear Scriptures to unclear Scriptures. [And in the process] the church guards the Scriptures; the Spirit guards the truth attested in Scripture."[16] For example, let's start with an *unclear* passage: John 4:10. Specifically, what is this 'gift of God' to which John is referring? When we reason by analogy, or compare other passages, such as, Acts 2:38, 8:18–20; 10:45; Jeremiah 2:13, 17:13; and John 7:37–39, we discover that the 'gift of God' is the Holy Spirit who is also referred to as "living water." Refer to Appendix A for the actual steps to discover that John equates the 'gift of God' with 'living water.'

Knowing the meaning of first fruits in Leviticus 23:9–14 aids us in understanding Paul's use of the phrase "first fruits" in 1 Corinthians 15:20. The feast of first fruits celebrated the first crops but it also celebrated the idea that more crops were to come and be harvested. Paul then uses first fruits in this way: Jesus' resurrection is to be celebrated for sure; however, His bodily resurrection assures more bodily resurrections are yet to come. Remember: the best and most reliable commentary on the Holy Scriptures are the Holy Scriptures!

HP#9: Interpreting God's Word requires humility.

The prophet Isaiah wrote in Isaiah 55:8-9 that God's thoughts are *higher than* our thoughts—think stratospherically higher. Now consider what the author Chesterton, says, "the poet [the Christian who uses his or her mind and imagination] only asks to get his head into the heavens. It is [the rationalist] who seeks to get the

---

15. Oden, *Rediscovering the African Seedbed*, 128.

16. Ibid., 128.

heavens into his head. And it is his head that splits."[17] Now juxtapose the prophet Isaiah's and Chesterton's words with the arduous task of biblical interpretation. What does this all mean? On one hand, we must do our due diligence in interpreting God's Word; however, on the other hand, because of our finiteness and fallenness, we should not be too proud to humbly seek the help of other brothers and sisters, in the body of Christ, who are more adept at biblical interpretation. (Willfully and stubbornly refusing help is being prideful, and simply crazy!)

> HP#10. Hermeneutics is a means to an end; that end is responding to God with all the faith, love, worship, and obedience that He intends.

Biblical hermeneutics is a means to an end. That "end" is applying God's Word in all areas of our life—in the home, at the workplace, on the athletic field, in the neighborhood, in the grocer check out line, in the public square, and in foreign lands. This means of course: if I am interpreting Scripture for my own edification and admonition, I must allow the Bible to *tell me what to do*; if I am preaching, I must be willing to *tell people what to do*; and if I am teaching God's Word, then I must be willing and courageous to *tell people what to do*—because the "purpose of the Bible is to change life"[18] so that we respond with all the faith, love, worship and obedience that God deserves and intends.

Identifying a "Passage of Scripture" (POS)

The reader has noticed thus far that I have used the phrase "passage of Scripture." A "passage of Scripture" refers to one or more verses that convey a single and coherent thought: think of a passage of Scripture as a paragraph in an essay. For example, the epistle 1 Peter has one major theme. The Apostle Peter had a purpose in mind when he wrote this book, which can be summarized this

17. Chesterton, *Orthodoxy*, 13.
18. Adams, *Truth Applied*, 35.

way: "*Peter tells us what God honoring conduct looks like in the face of suffering.*" Each chapter, and each passage of Scripture in 1 Peter, supports this one major theme. A passage of Scripture, like a paragraph in a literary piece, further develops the author's main point. And like a paragraph, a passage of Scripture has a beginning and an ending.

As an illustration, consider 1 Peter 2:18-25. Notice what Peter does—he gives *general* instructions to *everyone* in 1 Peter 2:13-17 and then he transitions to giving *specific* instructions to *specific* social classes of people: servants/slaves in vv. 18-25 and to husbands and wives in 3:1-7. 1 Peter 2:18-25 admonishes servants who suffer unjustly to mimic the example of Christ, who also suffered unjustly. 1 Peter 2:18-25 is a unit or passage of Scripture and one of many units of Scripture in 1 Peter. As literature, all the books in the Bible are a compilation of literary units stringed together to convey a main theme.

How Do I determine the "bookends" of a "Passage of Scripture"?

The short (and long) answer is read . . . read . . . and read. As we "sit" with a passage of Scripture, we will begin to discern the natural and intended breaks in the author's train of thought and thus, discover the natural limits or bookends of a passage of Scripture. Another way to think about this is, as we read we will begin to *see* the author's mental outline. However, the first thing to ask is, "how do I know I have a distinct passage of Scripture?" There are several things you can do, for instance:

1. Make note of the vocabulary of the passage of Scripture. For instance, in 1 Corinthians 5:1-13, the words, "sexual immorality" are repeated several times. So, the repetition of a word or phrases is an indication that you are studying a distinct or unitary passage of Scripture (POS).

2. Look for transitional words like "therefore," "finally," "now," "so," etc. For example, Paul uses the word "now" in 1 Corinthians 7:25, 8:1 and again in 12:1 to signal a new thought and thus, a distinct passage of Scripture. Likewise, the author of Ruth similarly uses the word "then" to mark a transition to a new thought. James signals a new thought by asking a rhetorical question (see and compare James 2:14, 3:13, 4:1 and 5:13, for example.)

3. Outlining a book or a chapter is also a helpful way to locate the bookends of a passage of Scripture.

My godson was quite an accomplished trumpet player in high school, he earned the coveted first chair in his school orchestra. If we were to ask him, how did you ascend to the first chair? He would likely answer unhesitatingly—it was the result of practicing . . . practicing and practicing. Likewise, you, the interpreter, will grow in your competency in identifying a passage of Scripture by practicing, practicing, and practicing.

You will notice that I will occasionally use "text" for "passage of Scripture" (POS) and vice versa.

My Favorite Quotes

Cultural icon, Oprah Winfrey, had a very popular segment on her TV Show called "Oprah's Favorite Things." Typically, this list of favorite things was aired around the Christmas holiday season. Even though the show is off the air, I still vividly remember some of her favorite things. In like fashion, let me conclude this chapter with a few of my favorite, yet poignant, quotes about interpreting the Bible:

- "The revelation of an infinite God by its nature must be complex, multifaceted and challenging to the human mind."[19] The idea of an infinite God and my finite, fallen human mind serves as a reminder to me that I should expect to "roll up

19. Veith, *God's Word*, 36.

my sleeves" and work to find God's intended meaning of the Bible.

- "We are dealing with God's thoughts: we are obligated to take the greatest pains to understand them truly and to explain them clearly."[20] The notion that I am "dealing with God's thoughts" causes me goose bumps! God has entrusted His thoughts to Me! I am, therefore, obligated to do my best, with the assistance of the Holy Spirit (of course), to understand His thoughts and to explain His thoughts clearly.

- "It is not sound hermeneutics to interpret an ancient text through the lens of any modern ideology, regardless of the social value of that ideology. The interpreter must respect the concerns of the author of [the book], which were indigenous to his own times and culture, not ours."[21] I do not like someone to take what I say out of context; similarly, if I disregard the context and author's concern, I run the risk of taking God's Words out of context!

- "Unless we recognize the 'distance' that separates us from the text [passage of Scripture] being studied, we will overlook differences of outlook, vocabulary, interest; and quite unwittingly we will read our mental baggage into the text without pausing to ask if that is appropriate."[22] (Note: to 'read our mental baggage into the text' is an illustration of eisegesis.) And this quote is similar, "The further removed the audience (us) is from the time and place of composition, the greater the difficulty in interpreting meaning. The gap is a special problem in Biblical interpretation."[23] I once told my Biblical Hermeneutics class that I come to the Bible as a foreigner, as the Bible original languages are foreign to me and the customs, dress, and rituals are all foreign to me. I am a foreigner because of the distance in time and space that separates me

20. Carson, *Exegetical Fallacies*, 15.

21. Jobes, *Esther*, 73.

22. Carson, *Exegetical Fallacies*, 104.

23. Young, *New Testament Greek*, 6.

from the times of the Bible. If I fail to recognize myself as a foreigner, I could very easily read my "mental baggage" into the sacred text.

I hope that, at the very least, these quotes cause you to pause and ponder the enormity or importance of the Biblical interpretation task. The stakes are extremely high when interpreting God's words and thoughts. Thus, we need some hermeneutics principles to *discipline* our interpretative journey. I strongly encourage you to review this chapter frequently.

Before leaving this chapter, you are encouraged to make these HPs personal. For example, I often heard HP#2 expressed "Context is King" but I revised it to read "Context is Emperor"—the meaning and emphasis is the same however. Now, proceed to the next chapter, where you will be introduced to the first letter of *SCAR*, or Sit (or "Sitting Awhile").

Please note: this is not the time to reach for any resource helps; only reach for your Bible—that is, a formal equivalent of the Bible.

2

"Sitting" Awhile with the Passage of Scripture

"A Time for Listening"[1]

HAVE YOU EVER TRAVELED to the inconspicuous and rather obscure city of Pawnee, Oklahoma? I suppose I should ask, have you ever heard of Pawnee, OK? My family and I traveled to Pawnee frequently when my wife's aunt, Lillie, was alive. Pawnee is nearly 126 miles southeast of Wichita, KS. Perhaps, one of Pawnee's most notable 'claims-to-fame' is Chester Gould, the cartoonist who invented the Dick Tracy comic strip, who hails from this city. Pawnee is one of those cities whose downtown is relatively small. Blink, and you might miss it!

Life in Pawnee is slower when compared to a bustling city like St. Louis, MO. In general, people in Pawnee are not in a hurry but move at leisurely pace. When we visited Aunt Lillie, it was just understood that we would *sit awhile* . . . eat, talk, and listen. Aunt Lillie did most of the talking, and we did most of the listening and eating! I loved these occasional retreats to Pawnee away from the hurried and frenzied rat race of big city life. I actually looked forward to sitting and hearing Aunt Lillie's stories and her uniquely high pitched laugh. And I loved being a beneficiary of her warm hospitality, typically in the form of delicious home cooked meals.

1. Listed as a corporate worship practice in Metropolitan Missionary Baptist Church's Order of Worship, March 5, 2014.

Fellow exegetes, let me encourage you to slow down, *sit awhile*, and hear another story . . . the grand story on the pages of Scripture (both the Old and New Testaments). It bears repeating: *sit awhile* and *listen* to God recount His story!

[S]CAR: See, Hear, Pray and Touch

Rabbis in antiquity, like second century Rabbi Akiva, taught their disciples at *yeshivas*. The word, "*yeshiva*," means to sit, dwell, or remain.[2] Indeed, second century sages like Akiva warmly recommended "the practice of exiling oneself to a place in which the Torah is taught."[3] What's the connection between yeshiva and "S" or Sit in *SCAR*? Like the disciples who exiled themselves away to study the Torah, "Sit" here means to *sit awhile* and read, and exile yourself so that you may read and re-read a passage of Scripture multiple times. (And if the book, in which the passage of Scripture is located, is brief, read it several times too.) Develop a voracious appetite for God's word!

Read the passage of Scripture and/or chapter or book *out loud* several times. According to Revelations 1:1–3, we are blessed when we read aloud God's Word. Perhaps, the Ethiopian Eunuch in Acts 8:26–40 knew this intuitively, as the evangelist Phillip heard him reading a portion of Isaiah out loud.

Model another dear saint's practice when she read God's Word. I love a friend's story about this woman who was encouraged to make a list of unbelievers to pray for during a Billy Graham Evangelistic Crusade. After she died, my friend was shown her list. To his surprise, his name was on it. My friend tells me that when this woman read the Bible she *placed her finger on each word as she read it*. So, *sit awhile* and read the Bible slowly. Read it aloud, and consider placing your finger on each word as you read it. And remember, you will benefit another way—as you read the passage several times you will also be memorizing the passage. Reading

2. Bobo, *Second Century Rabbi*, 106.
3. Ibid.

a passage of Scripture several times enables memorization which effectively "hides the Word in our heart" (Psalm 119:11).

Another practice I exercise when I *sit* with a text is to convert the text into a prayer. For example, when I read 2 Kings 22:18-19, a passage in which the prophetess assures King Josiah that his life will be spared, I prayed this immediately after, "Lord, I want a heart that is penitent and humbled before you." Similarly, when I read Titus, I beseeched the Lord, "to help me to be a "lover of good," "self-controlled," "upright," and "disciplined" and to show me in all respects how to be a "model of good works" and "in my teaching" to help me to "show integrity, dignity and sound speech" (see Titus 1:8, 2:7–8).

My colleague, Dr. Robert Smith, Associate Professor of Divinity Christian Preaching at Beeson Divinity School (Birmingham, AL) often encouraged his students to read the entire book, in which the passage of Scripture under consideration was a part, at least fifty times! I required my students to read the Biblical book at least twenty times.

Regardless, sit and read the passage of Scripture and/or book many times. You have permission to "cheat" too; that is, listen to an audio recording of your Biblical passage. Listen to the Bible as you exercise, or as you commute to work. The idea here is to immerse yourself in God's word.

Why read the passage of Scripture several times? Consider a former morning show KSDK-TV news reporter, Art Holliday, who writes, "When you're entrusted with telling someone's life story, that's a big responsibility."[4] We *sit* with the passage of Scripture to assure that we are actually hearing what God is saying. We too, have a big responsibility in telling God's story. So, *sit* and read the passage of Scripture many times.

Put your God given senses to work: *see* the passage of Scripture, *touch* each word of the passage of Scripture, and *hear* the passage of Scripture. And *pray* the Scripture!

---

4. Groshong, "Rock 'n' Roll Holliday," 50.

Record First Impressions

What should you do as you *sit* awhile with the passage of Scripture? As you *sit* awhile with the passage of Scripture, record your first impressions. Sometimes your first impressions will generally be correct. For example, a dear sister in Christ read through the book of Judges and her first impression was, "those folks were out of control!" Believe it or not, her initial impression was right on target! In fact, we might say the Israelites' out of control-ness was sadly cyclical and nauseating . . . like a merry-go-round as Figure 1 illustrates.

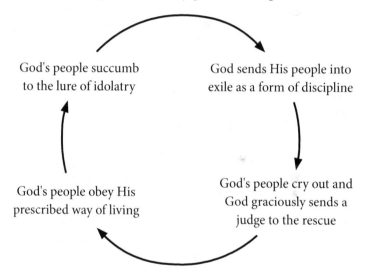

God's people succumb to the lure of idolatry

God sends His people into exile as a form of discipline

God's people obey His prescribed way of living

God's people cry out and God graciously sends a judge to the rescue

Figure 1. Obedience-Disobedience Cycle

Walk away after reading the minor prophet Micah, and you might think you have just read some court proceedings. And, this would be true, as certain portions of Micah read as God's people giving their defense and God, acting as a prosecutor, cross-examining His people and rendering His verdict. The book of Ruth reads, at first glance, like a love story . . . and in fact, it is. Specifically, the book of Ruth is referred to as a novella, or romance short story. However, and ultimately, as true of all narratives, God emerges as the hero of

37

this story. In the end, this story is about God's kindness and mercy expressed to Naomi, a bereft widow.

The message here: jot down your snap judgments of the Scripture as you read. However, remember that your first impressions are just that: first impressions! Our first impressions are like an unproven hypothesis. Your continued research will either prove or disprove your hypothesis. We must continue to tease out these first impressions and adequately judge them as either true or false. This is done as we proceed methodically through the letters from *S* to *C* to *A* to *R*.

Curiously Interrogate

As you sit with and read our passage of Scripture, *interrogate* the passage of Scripture. Be like the lovable Curious George[5] who was driven by his childlike curiosity to ask questions and to explore. Why ask questions? Questioning not only aids the development of critical thinking, but questioning allows you to enter into a dialogue with the Biblical author. Questions are also the gateway to learning. Authors (and educators), Postman and Weingartner, say it much more eloquently, "knowledge is produced in response to questions. And new knowledge results from the asking of new questions; quite often new questions about old questions. Here is the point: once you have learned how to ask questions—relevant and appropriate and substantial questions—you have learned how to learn and no one can keep you from learning whatever you want or need to know."[6] Wow, what a statement!

Learning to ask questions of the Biblical text will enable you to learn the Biblical text. Channel George's curiosity and jot down questions that arise as you read. Chances are, if you are teaching or preaching this text, you will raise questions that your audience may also have. You should prioritize your list and answer these

---

5. Curious George, the main protagonist of a series of popular children's books by the same name, were written by Hans Augusto Rey and Margret Rey.

6. Postman and Weingartner, *Subversive Activity*, 23.

questions. Some questions must be answered, start with those first. Other questions need not be answered at all.

How to Prioritize Your Questions

I follow these general guidelines when prioritizing my questions:

1. Consider your own context: if it is for an audience of one (namely, you), you can take your sweet time in answering these questions; however, if your audience is larger, think about those questions that will be most helpful to this audience.

2. Consider what the entire story of the Bible says. Or, consider what God has already said about the matter.

3. Consider rare words or phrases in the passage.

4. Consider words that appear multiple times.

5. Consider what questions Bible commentators ask and answer. (You will reach for a Bible Commentary later but once you use a commentary a few times, you will get a sense of what questions need to be answered and which ones can be placed on the back burner.)

For an example of questions, consider my list of questions from Ruth, Chapter 1 in Figure 2. Let's prioritize this list of questions. Now let's assume I am studying or teaching on Ruth 1:1–5.

After applying my general guidelines to these questions, I will seek to answer initially:

*   Questions #2, #3 and #5 because all these questions adhere to guideline (2) above. Notice these questions deal with Moab, and the entire Biblical narrative. For instance, Moab was a forbidden country for the Israelites (see Deuteronomy 7:1–5).

*   Question #6: because it adheres to guideline (2) above. We know from Old Testament books such as Deuteronomy (10:18), Isaiah (1:17), Exodus (22:22) and Psalms (68:5) that widows were in that group that God commanded care for.

39

- Question #7: because it adheres to guideline (4) above. The word "son" appears twice in these five verses.

Indeed, prioritizing a list of questions takes trial and error. Consulting Bible Commentaries will hone this skill too because we will be privy to the questions commentators ask and answer. And the good news is that at this point, we are early in the process of *SCAR* so we can hold our prioritized list lightly because our priorities may change.

Figure 2. Questions (and Commentary) Generated After Reading the Book of Ruth, Chapter 1

1. Narrator tells us when this story takes place: "when the *judges ruled . . .* " (vs. 1)

2. Was it okay for Elimelech to take his family to Moab? Was he just being a responsible protector/provider?

3. Where is Moab?

4. Why the detail that Elimelech was an Ephrathite? What does Elimelech's name mean?

5. Was it okay for Elimelech's sons to take wives from Moab? Did Ruth and Orpah become followers of Yahweh before they were married? No grandkids for Naomi for 10 years.

6. We are not told how Elimelech or his sons die but we have 3 widows. How were widows treated in this culture?

7. "Sons" in vs. 2 and vs. 5—is the same word for "son" being used?

8. What does Naomi's name mean? How did Naomi hear about the Lord visiting his people? (vs 6)

9. What is meant by "they lifted up their voices"? (vs. 9; also vs. 14)

10. Naomi is cynical ("if I should say I have hope"—vs. 12) and she is bitter toward God (vs. 13); 'the hand of the Lord has

gone out against me'—okay to be honest about our suffering—God can handle it!

11. Ruth clung to Naomi—means what? (vs. 14)

12. Ruth refuses to go back to her people and her gods; she makes Naomi's people and God, her people and God. Ruth forsakes her culture, family ties, and her gods. Ruth becomes a believer in Yahweh (vv. 15-18).

13. Main characters become: Naomi and Ruth; eventually Ruth and Boaz.

14. When Naomi and Ruth step into Bethlehem, "the whole town was stirred"? (vs. 19)

15. Again, Naomi expresses her bitterness toward God: don't call me Naomi ('pleasant') but refer to me as Mara (bitterness) (vv. 20-21); Naomi went away 'full' but because of the Lord, she has returned "empty"; what does it mean to say, "the Lord has testified against me"?

16. Is their return at the 'beginning of barley harvest' significant? (vs. 22)

See Appendix B for the remaining questions I generated while *sitting* with and reading Ruth, Chapters 2–4.

Pull Up a Chair and Imagine

It is time to pull up your comfortable chair and take a seat. If you so desire, reach for your favorite beverage as well, as you *sit awhile* with God's Word. Indeed, while you have permission to reach for your favorite beverage, this is *not* the time to reach for your favorite Biblical commentary. Don't be in a hurry to see what others have said about your passage of Scripture; rather, engage your heart, mind, and imagination. Read and re-read the passage of Scripture and allow the Holy Spirit to reveal God's thoughts to you. A colleague, Denis Haack, Director of Ransom Fellowship, is fond of saying this: give another person the "gift of unhurried time." Give the Bible the "gift of [your] unhurried time."

Imagine being part of the story as you read the passage of Scripture. Imagine being in the belly of the fish with Jonah. *Imagine* the opulence of Solomon's home, and his gold covered ivory throne. *Imagine* the revolutions per minute (RPM) of David's sling before that stone dislodged, traveled, and delivered its fatal blow to Goliath. *Imagine* being on the countryside as Jesus delivered His Sermon on the Mount. *Imagine* witnessing the Red Sea parting and walking on the dry sea bottom to the other side. Pray that you read the passage afresh as though you were reading it for the first time.

Dr. Robert Smith said, "Familiarity of the Bible can be an enemy of understanding the bible."[7] (See Hermeneutical Principle #6, in Chapter 1). "It is all too easy to read traditional interpretations we have received from others into the text of Scripture."[8] Sequester what you think you know about the passage of Scripture or book and "let the story wash over you again."[9] As you sit, interrogate the passage of Scripture and jot down your questions and thoughts.

Two Overarching Questions

The Heidelberg Catechism,[10] Question #2 asks: "What must you know to live and die in the joy of this comfort?"[11]

---

7. Dr. Robert Smith, Guest Lecturer for the Covenant Theological Seminary J. R. Wilson Preaching Lectures, Fall 2005.

8. Carson, *Exegetical Fallacies*, 17.

9. Doriani, *Getting the Message*, 68.

10. Ecumenical Creeds and Reformed Confessions, 13.

11. The 'comfort' spoken of here points to The Heidelberg Catechism, Question #1 which asks, What is your only comfort in life and in death? *Ans.* That I am not my own, but belong—body and soul, in life and in death—to my faithful Savior Jesus Christ. He has fully paid for all my sins with His precious blood, and has set me free from the tyranny of the devil. He also watches over me in such a way that not a hair can fall from my head without the will of my Father in heaven; in fact, all things must work together for my salvation. Because I belong to Him, Christ, by His Holy Spirit, assures me of eternal life and makes me wholeheartedly willing and ready from now on to live for Him. See Ecumenical Creeds and Reformed Confessions, p. 13.

Answer. Three things: first, I must know how great my sin and misery are; second, I must know how I am set free from all my sins and misery; third, I must know that I am to thank God for such deliverance.

This answer leads to the two interpretative questions you are to keep in the forefront of your mind, as your read any passage of Scripture:

1. What aspect of the human condition is revealed in this passage? Or, from Heidelberg Catechism Question #2, how does this passage show me 'how great my sin and misery are'? For instance, is the Biblical author discussing such sins as pride, or our propensity to worry, or our inclination to being discontent, etc.?

2. What is God's gracious remedy for *this* human condition? Or, again from the Heidelberg Catechism Question #2, how does this passage show me 'how I am set free from all my sins and misery'?

Why these two questions? As Figure 3 depicts, it is often at the intersection of the answers to Question #1 and Question #2 that we discover the meaning of the text. We will travel to this intersection when we discuss "R" of *SCAR* or the *Redemptive Remedy* in Chapter 5.

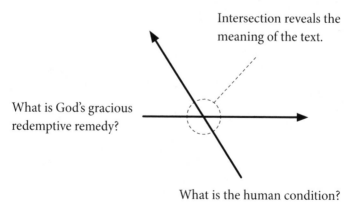

Figure 3. Meaning is Found at the Intersection

Can You Dig It?

Colleagues of mine have traveled to Abila, once known as the Decapolis[12] east of Jordan, to participate in archaeological digs. The excavation of such sites is instructive as this work helps us to better understand the various cultural landscapes of the Old and New Testaments and of the early church. However, my colleagues would readily admit that archaeological work is meticulously hard, arduous, and delicate. The work is especially hard because of the scorching summer sun. The work is painstakingly slow because archaeologists must dig carefully, and slowly, and often in small areas. However, the discovery of such treasures as small fragments of pottery, or weaponry makes the work worthwhile. Digging at archaeological sites such as Abila is similar to Biblical hermeneutics: it is slow, hard work "to dig" to understand such ancient literature as the Bible. However, the discovery of its true meaning makes the work worthwhile and quite rewarding.

12. See Mark 5:1–10; Matthew 4:24–25; Mark 7:31–37.

3

Context

"Texts are ***impoverished*** when they are taken out of that context
and interpreted in isolation."

—Timothy C. Tennent, *Invitation to World Missions*, p. 129

IN THE LAST CHAPTER, we were introduced to "S" of *SCAR* or the
need to "sit" awhile with the passage of Scripture, or Biblical book.
In this chapter, we consider the "C" in "SCAR"; the Context and
its *vital importance*. However, before plunging into the depths of
context and its significance, read the following text below from my
niece, Courtney "scrub"[1] (Figure 4).

---

1. I affectionately refer to her as "scrub" because as an older man, I beat her
in a 100 yard dash. Or let's just say, this is my version of "trash talking."

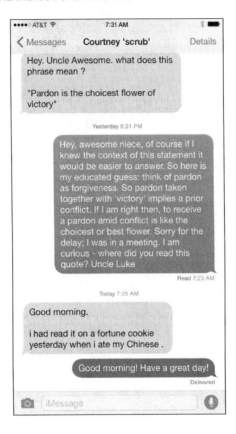

Figure 4. What's the Context?

Notice how I responded before knowing that this phrase was in a fortune cookie, "of course, if I knew the *context* it would be easier to answer. So here is my *educated guess*." The same can be applied to the task of interpreting the Bible. That is, *without knowing* the context, I am simply making an educated guess of what a passage of Scripture means, and as this chapter's introductory quote by Tennent mentions, "Texts are *impoverished* when they are taken out of that context and interpreted in isolation."[2]

If I were to simply say, "25" to someone, I would expect a blank stare. However, if I said "25 inches" to someone, I would

2. Tennent, *Invitation to World Missions*, 129.

envision the person's facial expression would change, because the units add specificity or context. Similarly, what if I said, "robot" and asked you to define or interpret it for me. You might guess and say, "a robot is a machine operated and guided by a computer like the beloved robot, R2-D2, in the film, *Star Wars* or similar to the robot WALL-E in the film by the same name." This would be a good guess, but that is all it is: an educated guess. Yet, you could not answer this question confidently and accurately without knowing the context. For instance, if we were located in America, this is likely what I had in mind; however, if we were located in in Cape Town, South Africa, this would not be what South Africans would have in mind. In South Africa, the traffic light (another electro-mechanical machine) is considered a "robot"!

Attempting to interpret something, whether that something is a robot or a passage of Scripture, without the benefit of knowing the context, is equivalent to interpreting *it* in isolation—which results in an impoverished response. I hope you see the implication: if we interpret passages of Scripture isolated from their context, we cheat ourselves and those to whom we teach or preach. This chapter takes up the important subject of context. Remember HP#2 is "Context is Emperor." Specifically, we need to thoroughly understand the literary, and cultural-historical contexts, to progress toward discovering the meaning of a passage of Scripture.

Literary Context

As mentioned in Chapter 1, the literary context asks, how do the verses that encompass our passage of Scripture (and the book of which this passage is a part) shed light on our chosen passage of Scripture?

Literary Context Analysis: The Upshot

The benefits of literary context analysis are several-fold: first, a thorough examination of the literary context (and the cultural-historical context) serves as our *on ramp* to analysis. Remember the Bereans? They examined what Paul said in Acts 17:10–15; where "examine" means to "sift up and down, *make careful* and *exact research* as in legal processes in the Scriptures for themselves."[3] As we do our literary context analysis, we are "sifting up and down" the Scriptures to arrive at an understanding. Think of the literary and cultural-historical contextual analysis as a panoramic or "wide angle" view. (Chapter 4, *Analysis,* will introduce us to a microscopic detailed analysis of the passage of Scripture.)

Second, by reading the passage of Scripture along with the surrounding verses, we are granted a special "access pass" inside the author's head and thus, are able to follow his logical train-of-thought. Many writers begin with an outline; the literary context analysis allows us to peek at the Biblical authors' outline.

Finally, as we read the passage of Scripture, and the surrounding verses and the Biblical book, we begin to see how our unitary passage fits within the larger context of the chapter and/or the book. As an added bonus, as we do the literary context analysis, we will begin to see the relationship between adjoining literary units.

For example, consider Figure 5. This diagram illustrates the import of analyzing the literary context. Literary context analysis looks backwards at the verses that come *before* the passage of Scripture; and it looks forward to the verses that come *after* the passage of Scripture. For example, the passage, Luke 17:20–18:8 clarifies our understanding of the verses that come next: Luke 18:9–14; and likewise, the passage Luke 18:15–19:10 explains the previous verses, Luke 18:9–14.

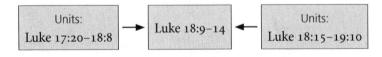

Figure 5. Literary Context Analysis Looks Forward *and* Backwards

3. Robertson, *Word Pictures,* 314.

Specifically, using an outline, Luke 17:20–18:8 can be summarized as follows:

- *Luke 17:20–37.* The Kingdom of God (KOG), while future, is also *present* in the person and work of Jesus Christ (17:21); but first things first, Christ must suffer death and be rejected by men (17:25). The KOG, that Christ will usher in, will be visible (17:24); and the KOG will come while many will be pre-occupied like those of Noah's and Lot's day.

- *Luke 18:1–8.* The righteous Judge, God, will mete out justice to the just (and to the unjust) on judgment day (another reference to the coming of the KOG); in the meantime, pray, or demonstrate our faith, day and night.

Similarly, using an outline, Luke 18:15-19:10 might summarized as follows:

- *Luke 18:15–17.* We must receive the Kingdom of God (Christ's Lordship) as children receive Jesus—"readily, trustingly and personally."[4]

- *Luke 18:18–30.* Jesus invites a rich young ruler (RYR) to KOG discipleship; yet as Jesus engages with him, the RYR discovers that his first priority *is not* the KOG, but rather his riches. After RYR's departure, Jesus teaches His disciples on the relationship between discipleship and riches.

- *Luke 18:31–34.* Jesus once again predicts His passion—His beating, flogging, scourging; His crucifixion, death and resurrection (see also Luke 5:35; 9:22, 44; 12:50; 13:32 and 17:25). Jesus' passion must occur before the future KOG is ushered in.

- *Luke 18:35–43.* Jesus performs work to prove that the KOG was in the people's midst (see Luke 17:21); and unlike the RYR's polite address (18:18), this blind beggar approaches Jesus with a confession, "Jesus, Son of David."

---

4. Ellis, *New Century Bible*, 216.

- *Luke 19:1–10.* Again, by saving Zacchaeus, Jesus performs work indicative of the KOG; and unlike the RYR, whose first priority was his riches, Zacchaeus relinquishes his grip on riches and gives more than the law required to make restitution for his prior fraudulent activity.

Notice what this outlining, or literary context analysis, tells us: these passages relate the present and future reality of the KOG (*Luke 17:20–37*) to *what* we should do in the meantime: pray (*Luke 18:1–8*) to *how* to receive the KOG, Christ's Lordship (*Luke 18:15–17*) to *how* putting Christ first is needed for entry into KOG discipleship (*Luke 18:18–30*) *to what* must occur before the future KOG arrives (*Luke 18:31–34*) *to what* KOG work looks like (*Luke 18:35–43* and *Luke 19:1–10*).

Luke 18:9–14 fits within this literary context of Luke 17:20–19:10, as in Luke 18:9–14 Jesus teaches us proper KOG behavior: to humble ourselves, in prayer, before a Holy God. Luke 18:9–14, therefore, defines entry into the Kingdom of God (KOG) and the corresponding KOG behavior.

"Naked Verses"

A "naked verse" is one that is lifted from its "rich and complex [literary] context"[5]; improperly clothed verses are not only vulnerable, but are susceptible to being misinterpreted and misapplied. Many of us have been privy to "naked verses." John 3:16 is commonly displayed at athletic events. At the time of this writing, travel I-35 North from Wichita, KS to Emporia, KS and a motorist will notice a placard near the 124 mile marker which reads, "Righteousness exalts a nation, but sin is a disgrace to any people" (Proverbs 14:34). Without the benefit of the verses that surround John 3:16 and Proverbs 14:34, it is everyone's guess what these two verses were truly intended to mean. Remember our poster child for a "naked verse" from Chapter 1? 1 Corinthians 15:33. Attempting to interpret a single or naked verse devoid of its rich context is futile and quite unwise. The Bible is

5. Butterfield, *The Secret Thoughts*, 67.

not unique in this regard. That is, if you do not consider the literary context in any literary piece is folly. Consider this *single* or 'naked' line from the wonderful children's book, *Velveteen Rabbit*:[6]

> "Real isn't how you are made," said the Skin Horse.

Now, what if I asked you to give me the meaning of Skin Horse's statement? Actually, you could not, because this single statement is bereft of its context; we need the other sentences around it to arrive at the meaning. Let's clothe this "naked" statement with the sentences around it:

> "What is REAL?" asked the Rabbit one day, when they were laying side by side near the nursery fender, before Nana came to tidy the room. "Does it mean having things that buzz inside you and a stick-out handle?"
> *"Real isn't how you are made," said the Skin Horse.* "It's a thing that happens to you. When a child loves you for a long, long time, not just to play with, but REALLY loves you, then you become REAL."
> "Does it hurt?" asked the Rabbit. "Sometimes," said the Skin Horse, for he was always truthful. "When you are Real you don't mind being hurt." "Does it happen all at once, like being wound up," he asked, "or bit by bit?"
> "It doesn't happen all at once," said the Skin Horse. "You become. It takes a long time. That's why it doesn't often happen to people who break easily, or have sharp edges, or who have to be carefully kept. Generally, by the time you are Real, most of your hair has been loved off, and your eyes drop out and you get loose in the joints and very shabby. But these things don't matter at all, because once you are Real you can't be ugly, except to people who don't understand."

Now, you can answer my question: Skin Horse is giving Rabbit a lesson on how one knows when he or she is real.[7] So, likewise, if

6. Williams, *Velveteen Rabbit*, 4–5.

7. When I taught on 'calling and identity,' I often used this dialogue between the Skin Horse and Rabbit to encourage Christians to locate their identity (worth) in Christ and in nothing else (our jobs, our pedigrees, our wealth, our intelligence, etc.).

1 Corinthians 15:33 was taken by itself, it would appear that this passage would justify staying clear of unbelievers. However, as Figure 6 illustrates, the verses before it, 1 Corinthians 15:29–32 and the verse after, 1 Corinthians 15:34 and, of course, the remaining verses in 1 Corinthians 15, offer us more clarity, and we discover that this verse is not grounds for shunning unbelievers. Rather, this verse is calling out those in the Corinthian church who are denying the bodily resurrection of Jesus Christ. And, consequently, they are labeled 'bad company' because their beliefs are producing bad morals.

Figure 6. Who is the "Bad Company"?

Four, as we labor in the field of doing the literary context analysis, we will be able to discern the meaning of words and phrases. As my example of the *Velveteen Rabbit* shows, we naturally discern the meaning of words in context. So, the literary context serves as the final arbiter of determining the meaning of a word.

Let's look at two examples of how the literary context serves to define words or phrases.

Example #1

What is the meaning of "Zion" in Isaiah 1:8? If we keep reading, the wider literary context affords us the answer. "Zion" is the same as Jerusalem (see 2:3 and 10:32). Again, as we progress through the steps of *SCAR*, our initial conclusions will be either affirmed or refuted.

Example #2

In Revelation 3:7–13 God addresses the "angel" of the church in Philadelphia. Who is this "angel"? And is this "angel" of the sort like the angel Gabriel? We find the same word in Revelation 2:1,

2:8, 2:12, 2:18, 3:1 and 3:14. And we find the plural form of the word in Revelation 1:20. Reading the passages around Revelation 3:7–13 as the literary context analysis instructs us, or reading Revelation 1:1–3:6 and Revelation 3:14–4:22, we can say preliminarily that "angel" in Revelation 3:7 refers to the leader of the church in Philadelphia.

The big idea with these two brief examples is the importance of reading around our passage of Scripture to arrive at the meaning of words and/or phrases.

Here are a few examples of how laboring to understand the literary context pays off:

a. *Were the disciples being pious or impious?* Disciples plead with Jesus in Luke 17:5 to "increase their faith!" Taken by itself, this seems like a godly and pious request; but here the disciples say it after they hear a difficult command (see Luke 17:1-4) and before Jesus tells them they merely need the faith of a mustard seed (see Luke 17:6). Considering the context and Jesus' mild rebuke in Luke 17:6, some interpreters have seen the apostles' request to "increase our faith" not as a godly request worth modeling but rather as an excuse.[8] Jesus wants His disciples to simply exercise the small faith that they have, which is capable of doing seemingly the impossible.

b. *How should we pray?* Whatever we ask in Jesus name in John 14:33, if taken by itself, can lend support of those who preach the prosperity gospel; however, when John 14:33 is taken with 1 John 3:22-23, we are reminded that what we ask must be according to His will.

c. *Why is God calling Abram so significant?* The horrific event recorded in Genesis 11:1-9 set up Genesis 12:1-3: the commissioning of Abram, as another Adam,[9] to be a conduit of blessings to the nations.

---

8. See Richard B. Vinson, *Gospel According to Luke*, Macon, GA: Smyth & Heylwys, 2008, p. 540 and Dan Doriani, *Getting the Message: A Plan for Interpreting and Applying the Bible*, Phillipsburg, NJ, 1996, p. 34.

9. We too are called to mimic the second Adam, Jesus Christ (see Romans 5).

d. *What role does Romans 12:1 serve?* Romans 12:1 serves as a fulcrum and only makes sense when we read and reflect on what Paul has masterfully written about the righteousness that comes by faith in Romans 3-11.

e. *Why did King David treat Saul's offspring with kindness?* 1 Samuel 18:1-3 and 2 Samuel 5:6-10 helps us to understand 2 Samuel 9:1-12. Read 2 Samuel 9:1-12 and then read 1 Samuel 18:1-3 and 2 Samuel 5:6-10. What do you see? In other words, the literary context can span many chapters and can also include another book. Similarly, to understand Genesis 15 we must look to Genesis 12-14 and Genesis 16-25 because these passages are largely about Abraham and his spiritual maturation.

f. *Who are the spiritual ones?* Galatians 6:1 states "brothers, if anyone is caught in any transgression, you who are spiritual should restore him." The natural question is, 'what does *spiritual* look like' or 'who are the spiritual ones'? Galatians 5:22-23, better known as the 'Fruit of the Spirit' answers that question. In other words, those who regularly produce the Fruit of the Spirit are the 'spiritual ones' and thus, are called upon to restore a wayward brother or sister. We only know this if we read Galatians 5; or we only know this if we diligently consider the literary context.

g. *Have we seen Paul do this before?* In 1 Corinthians 13:1-3 Paul uses the first person pronoun "I." The literary context analysis informs us that Paul has done this before—that is, used himself as an example of proper behavior. For example, see 1 Corinthians 9 and count the number of instances where he uses "I."

Pardon me, but I failed to mention something—make this Hermeneutical Principle #11: Bible interpreters must absolutely love reading the Bible! Literary Context Analysis demands this love of reading the Bible. And I guarantee as you interpret each passage of Scripture, passages that you have read before, and that link in some fashion with your passage of Scripture, will suddenly register in your mind. How can I make this guarantee? God wants to be known . . . so He works with His Word and with the Holy Spirit to politely barge into our hearts and minds!

A Final Word about Words

Words are used to create literature. No words, no literature. The exegete must pay attention to words. Words are important in the Bible (which is also literature). Some lessons about words:

1. Words change meaning over time. For example, we often use the word 'nice' to describe a person who is pleasant. Centuries ago, in Latin speaking contexts, to call someone "nice" would have been equivalent to calling the person, "ignorant."

2. Words have different meanings across languages. Take my last name, "Bobo" for example. In *Portuguese*, "Bobo" means 'fool' or 'silly'—because of this, when I was invited to lecture and preach in Brazil in Summer 2007, my host suggested I go by the name, "Luke Brad" (Brad is my middle name); my former Graduate Assistant (or GA) told me with a wide grin on her face, that "Bobo" means "kiss" in her native *Haitian creole* language; in *French*, my last name was once spelled, Beaubeaux, which means 'beautiful beautiful.' If my last name has different meanings across different languages, the same holds true for words in the Bible, which were originally of Hebrew, Aramaic, and Greek origin.

3. Many English words have a wide range of meanings (or semantics). Likewise, many Hebrew and Greek words have a wide range of meanings too. For example, the word "covenant" could mean a friendship covenant (see 1 Samuel 18) but this covenant can be equally broken because it is between two equals; however, the "covenant" God makes with man is not between equals and while we may break our covenant vows, God never breaks His. Consider the word, "man." In 1 Timothy 2:12, we are take the meaning of the word literally as "man" but the same word means "husband" in Matthew 1:16.

4. Consider the word "burden" in Galatians 6:1-5. There are two occasions where the word 'burden' is used in this passage; however, while they are spelled the same, they are two different words in Greek, and they mean two different things too.

The final word on words . . . is I invite you to become a *logophile*—a person who loves words, especially Biblical words. And I caution you *not to assume* a word in the Bible carries the same meaning of the word in your native language.

Wider Literary Context

It is worth mentioning that Biblical interpreters must not only consider the verses that surround the passage of Scripture under examination but also the "wider literary context" of Scripture. We should consider not only the book in which the passage of Scripture is recorded, but we should also consider the *entire testament* in which the passage of Scripture is found. For example, let's look at Genesis 11:1–9 together. To get the full benefit of the literary context, we should consider the surrounding verses that sandwich Genesis 11:1–9 and also the wider literary context of the book of Genesis, as well. See Figure 7 which illustrates this.

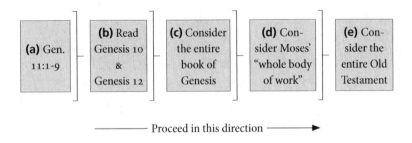

Figure 7. Old Testament Passage Couched Within Its Wider Literary Context

Explanation:

a. Genesis 11:1-9 is a classic example of human hubris on display.

b. Genesis 10 and Genesis 12 envelop Genesis 11:19; Genesis 10 lists the Table of Nations; the result of scattering the people in Genesis 11:1-9; and Genesis 12 begins with God commissioning Abram, the second Adam, to be a blessing to the nations which are result of Him scattering them.

c. Genesis 18:21 relates another time when "God came down" and believe me, this *was not* a pleasant visit.

d. Moses wrote the first five books of the Bible or the Pentateuch, so consider these books as well. Again, this comes under the HP #8, *Scripture interprets Scripture*.[10]

e. Consider the entire Old Testament.

Next, consider this example from the New Testament, Figure 8:

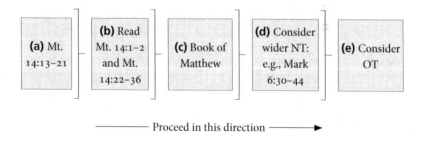

Proceed in this direction ⟶

Figure 8. New Testament Passage within Its Wider Literary Context

---

10. This same principle of considering an author's 'whole body of work' would apply to any author who wrote more than one of the Biblical books (e.g., Paul, John, Peter, etc.).

Explanation:

a. Matthew re-telling of Jesus feeding the 5,000 men not count-ing women and children.

b. These passages envelop our passage of Scripture.

c. Compare this account with another mass feeding in Matthew 15:32-39.

d. Here we consider the other gospel accounts because again, HP #8, *Scripture interprets Scripture*. The Gospel account ac-cording to Mark adds a small detail, "He commanded them to sit down in groups on the green grass" (vs. 39).

e. Jesus' feeding the 5,000 is reminiscent of God feeding the multitude with manna in Exodus 16:35. Jesus' work and min-istry mirrors His Father's work and ministry.

One final example. Consider 2 Kings 2:6-8 and Figure 9. This passage of Scripture recounts the prophet Elijah miraculously parting the Jordan River so that he and his protégé, Elisha, might cross and continue their trek. "Parting a river" should sound fa-miliar to us—and the wider literary context says we are right.

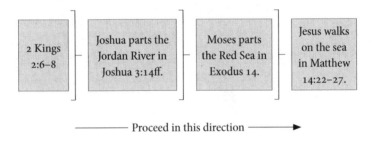

Figure 9. Old Testament Passage and Its Wider Literary Context

Genesis 1, among other places in Scripture, reminds us that God has created all things—visible and invisible. So, based on 2 Kings 2:6-8 and its cursory wider literary context, we can at least conclude: God is sovereign over all that He has created. God is sovereign over nature and that includes large bodies of water.

Cultural-Historical Context

Located in St. Louis, Missouri is the Museum of Transportation. This museum traces advancements in transportation from horse-drawn carriages to carriages with horsepower under the hood. The benefits of visiting museums are that we get an idea how people lived, played, and worked in the past. In many ways, we are transported back to a former time. By carefully examining the cultural-historical context of Scripture, we are entering a museum and by doing so, we get an idea how people of the Bible lived. Entering this museum of great riches is necessary because as one panelist put it, "we are not only reading words but we are reading a *culture*."[11] And these cultures are quite a distance from us. You might remember this quote from my favorite quotes in Chapter 1: "The further removed the audience (us) is from the time and place of composition, the greater the difficulty in interpreting meaning. The gap is a *special problem* in Biblical interpretation."[12] Note a few things from this quote:

First, while we are an audience, we are not the first or the intended audience; the Bible captures the actions, words, etc. in a specific time in history for specific audiences in history. This means we must labor to understand what the *first* audience heard and understood.

Second, closing the gap occurs at this stage of the interpretative process. Here, we ask about geography, modes of travel, rituals, customs, social conventions, the societal structure, dress, architecture, agriculture, family structure, and climate. We also ask, what was happening economically, militarily, politically, religiously, and philosophically? For example, a lost coin (the drachma) would have represented considerable buying power, or might have been

11. http://feedproxy.google.com/~r/refuge-church-podcast/~3/DEr_Uc7eR9U/20150607_Trey_1st.mp3.

12. Young, *New Testament Greek*, 6.

used as part of a headdress of a wedding outfit (see Luke 15:8–10). Thus, the first audience would have been quite interested in the outcome of this story. Or, another example, from architecture was a "parapet"—it was like a railing around the perimeter of a roof and was quite necessary as people in antiquity slept on the roof (see Deuteronomy 22:8 and 1 Samuel 9:26). So for liability purposes, homeowners were requested to install parapets (a railing) to preclude someone from rolling off the roof or falling off, if the guest engaged in sleepwalking.

Cultural-Historical Analysis: The Upshot

The benefits of examining the cultural-historical context is that one, we are transported back to a time foreign to us, and thus, we are able to make sense of practices, customs, etc. that seem strange to our modern notions and sensitivities. In this way, we examine how people lived, earned a living, parented, and made transactions.

And two, by closely studying the cultural-historical context we can avoid the temptation of reading our contemporary context—the meaning of its customs, word definitions, etc.—into this distant context because "unless we recognize the 'distance' that separates us from the text being studied, we will overlook differences of outlook, vocabulary, interest; and quite unwittingly we will read our mental baggage into the text without pausing to ask if that is appropriate."[13]

Another benefit of exploring the cultural-historical context is that we can begin to answer the questions we generated when we "sat" with the passage of Scripture.

Finally, the cultural-historical contextual analysis helps us to *situate* our passage in real human history. This analysis helps us to appreciate the people, events, and artifacts of the period of time where our passage of Scripture is located. This analysis disciplines us to not read a later period of redemptive history into a previous

13. Carson, *Exegetical Fallacies*, 104.

period of redemptive history and vice versa. Moreover, this analysis allows us to see the progress of God progressively and methodically unfolding His redemptive plan.

Here are some golden nuggets I unearthed after doing some cultural-historical context analysis:

- *Customs*: Judicial proceedings took place at the gate (see Ruth 4:1–11). Jesus' trial was at night—but was this legal or *illegal*? It was illegal and this explains the rushed trial meeting in Matthew 27:1–2 the following morning. The Samaritan woman in John 4 was a social outcast. How do we know that? For a hint, see Genesis 24:11: women came to the well early in the morning to beat the hot summer sun. Prophet Elijah tossed his cloak around Elisha not because he was cold but rather as a sign of the prophet's vocation; thus, throwing his cloak to Elisha was a symbol of Elisha's impending call to the prophetic office (see 1 Kings 19:19–21; compare to 1 Kings 19:15–18).

- *Rituals*: Jews were required to fast once a year during the Day of Atonement (*yom kippur*). This fact puts Luke 18:9–14 in perspective. Here the Pharisee was not praying but rather bragging about his "ritualistic piety"—"I don't fast once *a year* but *twice* a week (or 104 times a year)." God borrows covenantal practices from the existing pagan residents; and this explains God's maledictory oath ceremony in Genesis 15:1-21.

- *Dress*: Tamar dressed up as a 'prostitute' in Genesis 38:12–15 and takes her place by the road (see also Jeremiah 3:2); and in John 13, Jesus dons servant/slave attire before washing His disciples' feet, a job for a servant/slave. In other words, clothing pointed to one's social standing/occupation in society in antiquity.

- *Geography*: The placement of Israel (the land or nation) was providential as the land served as a "land bridge." So as traders/visitors/travelers passed from Africa to Syria, Tyre, etc. they would interface with the Israelites who were commanded to be a "light to the nations" (Isaiah 42:6). Refer to a map of Israel (see the back of your Bible).

- *Philosophically*: Philosophically, the audience at the Areopagus was diverse because in the audience were Epicureans, Cynics and Stoics. And most importantly, Paul chooses words and makes gestures appropriate for the audience to 'build a bridge' (see Acts 17:22-34).

- *Politically*: When Joshua and company conquered the "Promised Land" there was a power vacuum which means that the opposition was light to non-existent militarily and politically—which is certainly evidence that God had gone before His people. Although Jonathan (Saul's son) was the next in line to ascend the throne, Jonathan de-clothes and puts his garments on David (1 Samuel 18:1–4) and this signals divesture (Jonathan's self-removal from office) and the investiture of David.

- *Militarily*: Our sensitivities would regard the killing in Esther 9:1–19 as gratuitous and unnecessary. However, this was not gratuitous killing, but was rather accepted as normal warfare practices. Again another example from Esther will be instructive. King Xerxes held a seven day drinking festival and by so doing he was displaying the vast wealth of his kingdom. All of this, in the end, was done to secure the loyalty and support of his entire empire as they would soon engage in war against the Greeks. King Xerxes wanted to display one more piece of evidence of his power and glory: Vashti. But, although Vashti was summoned by the king, she refused to come. Vashti's blatant refusal, undoubtedly embarrassing to the king, sparked a question from a friend on Facebook. She asked why did Vashti not come when she was summoned by the king? She continues, "Was it a *cultural* thing? Maybe it was a testament to her character, and she was lazy, dispassionate or unkind?" She asked me to respond which I gladly did. My short answer was: yes, it was a *cultural* thing. My long answer was, "This king, also known as King Headache,[14] held great power; but he exercised it capriciously, thus making his decisions fraught with "dubious

---

14. Jobes, *Esther*, 36.

motives with impaired judgment."[15] The king wanted to flaunt his wealth, glory, and power to breed loyalty in his men who would later engage in war with the Greeks. Flaunting Vashti, his trophy wife, before his guests would have been another way to showcase his wealth and power. However, Vashti disobeyed the king and refused to come into the Persian Court because she knew it would not be safe because of King Xerxes' propensity to exercise his power willy-nilly and recklessly.

- *Religiously*: Israelites did not live in a benign religious context; rather, they lived in a religiously pluralistic society (if you are an American, a religiously pluralistic society should sound very familiar). Father Abraham was believed to be a henotheist—someone who believes in one God without denying the existence of other gods (see Joshua 24:1–2). Christians in the first century also lived in a religiously pluralistic time; in fact, many Roman Emperors, like Commodus, demanded to be worshiped as a deity.

- *Socially*: Socially structural wise, in the Greco-Roman world, the Roman emperor alone sat atop the social ladder while 'expendables' like cripples, beggars, criminals, widows, orphans pulled up the rear or were relegated to the bottom rung of society. This could explain why these expendables flocked to hear Jesus.

These many categories of cultural context really should not surprise you. Why? Because the Bible captures real people living in "modern" societies situated chronologically and geographically in history. In other words, just like we view our societies educationally, religiously, medically, technologically, politically, and economically, we can likewise view ancient societies educationally, religiously, medically, technologically, politically, and economically. On the other hand, maybe you are not surprised but you might be wondering where do I start? Should I consider what was happening religiously or medically? One way to solve this dilemma is to inspect

15. Ibid., 69.

your questions recorded during the *Sitting* stage. Allow these questions to serve as your on ramp for this particular analysis step.

A Sample Text

Let's look at a passage where many of these categories of cultural context are present. For example, consider Malachi 1:1-5.

- *Religiously,* God's people were spiritually destitute or lethargic. This explains why the priests offered blemished sacrifices and why the people made ethical compromises, such as rampant divorces and the negligent payment of tithes.

- *Economically and agriculturally,* the people were experiencing severe economic hardship because their crops were decimated by the "devourer"—a generic name for crop-destroying pests (Malachi 3:11).

- *Historically (and prophetically),* the temple, destroyed by the Babylonians, had been rebuilt (see Malachi 1:10; 3:1, 8 for allusions to the existence of the temple) and temple-worship had resumed. Thus, Malachi was a *post*exilic prophet or he lived and prophesied after the Babylonian captivity.

- *Politically,* although the exiles had returned from Babylon to a minor province in Judea, they were no longer ruled by a Davidic King (this is reminiscent of Judges 21:25); rather, they were still under limited rule (the term "governor" was often used for regional officials during the Persian period, 539–332 B.C.). Incidentally, without a king, these exiles were *militarily* vulnerable because kings often led their people into battle. And because the "king was expected to further religion"[16] this also explains the people's moral decadence.

These cultural-historical categories explain why the prophet Malachi begins his book by reminding God's people of His electing, covenantal love. In so doing, Malachi hopes to revive their

16. Douglas and Tenney, *The International Dictionary of the Bible,* 567.

indifferent hearts—moving them from disobedience and spiritual lethargy *to* obedience and spiritual vitality.

Conclusion

Hopefully, you, the reader, see the bounty of information that is reaped by doing the literary and cultural-historical contextual analyses. I used several tools—chief among these tools was the Holy Scriptures. Besides Scripture, I consult resources such as those listed in Appendix D. Reiterating, the benefits of examining the literary and cultural-historical contexts are numerous; thus, skipping this step is, indeed, unwise. By starting here, we begin a careful and exacting analysis of our passage of Scripture. Exploration of the literary and cultural-historical contexts prevents us from committing a common mistake—"quoting God's Word out of context"—and who wants the dubious honor of quoting or taking God's words out of context? The exploration of the literary and cultural-historical contexts closes the gap between times and cultures foreign to us and will afford many "ah-ha" moments.

4

Analysis

"A mind is a terrible thing to waste."

—UNCF

"STUDENTS, IT'S TIME TO put on our thinking caps." I remember many of my Kansas City elementary school teachers were fond of making this statement. This often was said, for instance, prior to doing a science or mathematics lesson (on second thought, teachers should have repeated the phrase prior to doing art and literature curriculum too). When it comes to the "A" of *SCAR* or Analysis, this is where we must don our thinking caps, too, as this is where Biblical hermeneutics, as the *science* of interpretation comes in to play.

Analysis Defined

The American Heritage Dictionary defines the word *analysis* this way: "the separation of an intellectual or material whole into its constituent parts for individual study."[1] Because "hermeneutics focuses on the details,"[2] our analysis must focus on the details— punctuation, sentence structure, direct and indirect objects, and genre. Good Bible interpreters look for *details,* and they are not in a hurry. For example, if we compare Mark's account of feeding the

1. The American Heritage Dictionary, 64.
2. Butterfield, 87.

5,000 (6:30–44), and Matthew's account (14:13–21), we find that Mark adds the inconspicuous detail of 'green grass' (vs. 39). After reading 1 and 2 Samuel, we notice another detail—the author's affinity for the word "hand."

Analysis, in hermeneutics, examines the many components of a passage of Scripture, to understand the whole passage of Scripture. Indeed, doing biblical hermeneutics on a passage of Scripture is a complex task; however, we can break down this arduous process into bite-size chunks, to better understand. Once we have dissected the whole into its parts, we can begin to arrive at the meaning of a text.

As we don our "thinking caps," remember that analysis demands that we sift through several reputable sources of information to arrive at sound and logical conclusions, and to make informed inference via research. Yes, to be a good Bible interpreter, means having an affinity for doing some research. Analysis in general, and Biblical interpretation in particular, takes discernment; and discernment means testing or evaluating our initial conclusions against what we know of God's character, His redemptive plan for His world, church history, the Bible, and our reality—all of which serves as our checks and balances. We should be suspicious of people (including ourselves) who say, "I have discovered a new meaning from this passage of Scripture." We are not the first to interpret God's Word, and our interpretation should line up with those who came before us.

Our "Hermeneutical Toolbox"

Thus far we have been introduced to two hermeneutical tools: literary context analysis and cultural-historical context analysis. In this chapter, I will introduce these additional tools:

a. Identifying the Genre

b. Literary Device Analysis

c. Word Studies

d. Other Tools

Starting Point: Identifying the Genre

Genre is, generally speaking, a literature type or form. Biblical authors used a variety of genres (or discourse types) appropriate, for their subject matter and audience, to tell the story of the Bible. Sometimes a piece of Biblical literature used one genre exclusively; while at other times, an author might have used several genres in one literary piece.

1 Samuel is an interesting case study. While this book belongs to the history genre, sometimes the subject matter within the book fits under another genre. For example, the narrator of 1 Samuel used praise poetry to express Hannah's joy and thanks to Yahweh for her son in 1 Samuel 2:1-10. Remember prior to this Hannah was barren and distraught. This idea of multiple genres in one book also explains the psalm and songs in Jonah 2 and Luke 1–2, respectively. Pictured in Figure 10 are the genres utilized in the Old Testament Scriptures: Prose, Prophecy, and Poetry. Prose is expressed as Law, Narrative, or History. Similarly, the Prophecy and Poetry genres can be expressed in additional forms as well.

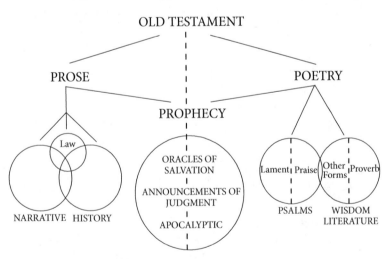

Figure 10. Cracking Old Testament Codes[3]

3. *Cracking Old Testament Codes.* Edited by D. Brent Sandy and Ronald IL. Giese, Jr. Nashville: Broadman & Holman, 1995, pp. 298.

Similarly, the literary genres utilized by New Testament authors are:[4]

- Narrative Literature (Gospels and Acts)
- Epistolary Literature (Paul's Letters and the general epistles like Hebrews and James)
- Apocalyptic Literature (Revelation)

While, all genres operate on our imaginations, emotions (hearts), intellects, and wills—they do so *differently*. Implication? When it comes to Biblical interpretation, we must analyze a passage of Scripture through the lens of its unique genre (or genres).

Proper analysis begins with identifying the genre of the passage of Scripture. The introduction of a Biblical commentary will often identify the genre or genres. (See Appendix D for suggested resources for your library).

Defining the genre helps us to determine the meaning of a passage of Scripture because often the *behavior* of the literature follows its *type*—poetry functions like poetry; narrative behaves like narrative; and an epistle functions like an epistle. Knowing the genre helps us to manage and discipline our expectations. For example, we cannot expect prose to function as poetry; and do not expect poetry to behave the same as epistolary literature.

The literature's genre (the form) also provides some idea of how that piece of literature functions. For example, we must *infer* principles from literature that is composed using narrative and history genres. For instance, one principle we can infer from 2 Samuel 9, which recounts David's kindness to Mephibosheth (son of Jonathan), is that God shows kindness despite our social status. Another principle we can draw from 2 Samuel 9, is that we all have a "seat at the table" in God's family. That is, in God's kingdom there are no big people and no little people as we all share equal worth and value.

The psalms are *poetry,* and like most poetry, the psalms make use of natural language in an artistic, emotive, and heightened

4. Adapted Agan's notes on *Semantic Genres.*

fashion. Thus, the exegete must tarry to understand the meaning behind a poet's highly figurative language. For example, Psalm 2 is considered a 'royal psalm' and when the congregation sang it, the psalm reminded them that God had exalted David and his descendants to be kings, in order for them to fulfill the very purpose for which Abraham was called—to be a conduit of blessings to the nations (see Genesis 12:1–3). So, it is in that light that "kiss the son" (vs. 12a) makes sense. Figuratively, "kiss the son," means to "obey him."[5]

Likewise, the Ten Commandments (or Decalogue) in Exodus 20:1–17 is of the form of law and, therefore, must be interpreted with this in mind. That is, as law, we can expect little to no ambiguity; when God says, "you shall not steal" in Exodus 20:15—that is unquestionably clear. However, there is more homework yet to do on a passage like Exodus 20:15: for instance, why do we have a propensity to steal and what does stealing reveal about the human heart?

Analyzing apocalyptic literature, such as certain portions of Daniel and the book of Revelation, will necessitate a careful and thorough interpretation of symbols and imagery. See Tables 2 and 3 at the end of this chapter for what to expect from a piece of literature based on its genre.

Authors' "Go To" Genre: Narrative

Over a third of the Bible fits nicely into the narrative genre, so clearly this was the "go to" genre for many of the Biblical authors and narrators. And, most narratives will follow the curve in Figure 11. When analyzing a narrative we ask questions:

- What is the setting for the story?
- Who are the major and minor characters?
- What is the plot?

5. Moseley, np.

- What is the resolution (or denouement or finale) to the problem?

In short, analyze a narrative per the diagram below.[6] Because a narrative is a story, a story has characters or actors that speak *and* act. When analyzing a narrative, then, we must look carefully at the characters' words *and* the actions. When we study the words spoken by a character, this is referred to as "discourse analysis." Consequentially, we must focus on *what is said, how it is said,* and *who said it* and/or on the actor's <u>actions</u>—*what was done* and *who did it.*

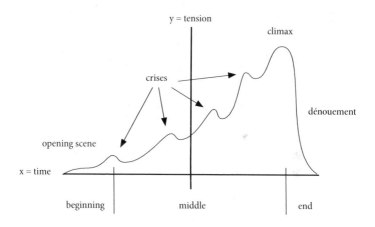

Figure 11. Topography of a Narrative

Using Figure 11

Let's apply the diagram in Figure 11 briefly to the book of Ruth. In the opening *scene*, the patriarch of the family, Elimelech moves his family from famine stricken Bethlehem to the country of Moab. Immediately, the story moves to a *crises* point: Naomi, a foreigner in Moab, bereft of not only her husband but her two sons, is now a *childless* widow. The story's *climax* occurs when Boaz, a relative

6. See http://www.musik-therapie.at/PederHill/Structure&Plot.htm.

of the deceased Elimelech, enters into negotiations with another relative of Elimelech, who has the first right to redeem the land belonging to Elimelech. When Boaz relates that buying the land means also acquiring the Moabite Ruth, this relative refuses to redeem the land. So, Boaz redeems the land and acquires and takes Ruth's hand in marriage. Finally, the *denouement* (or finale) occurs when Ruth gives birth to a son—which means a *childless* widow is now a grandmother.

Literary Device Analysis

A former student, while learning about the topic *historicist* criticism, kindly shared her class notes with me because the principles she was learning overlapped with Biblical hermeneutics. Under the word "guards" on her notes, she writes, "we can't read any text until we understand the conventions of the text; a text is like a musical score. Without conventions it's meaningless."[7] Summing up this lecture, she wrote this formula:

> "Conventions + context of speaker = understanding of meaning."

This is apropos for our discussion here. Substituting 'literary devices' for 'conventions,' I offer this revision to the formula:

> "Literary devices + context (literary and cultural-historical) = helps to understand the meaning of our passage of Scripture."

Biblical authors used a plethora of literary devices; thus, we must be on the lookout for them and understand them. Here is a representative sample of literary devices we can find in our Bibles:

a. *Hyperbole.* Matthew 5:30 has puzzled many lay persons. "And if your right hand causes you to sin, cut it off and throw it away. For it is better that you lose one of your members than that your whole body go into hell." This is an example of hyperbole, and is not to be taken literally. Just imagine if we took

7. Mueller, *ENG 45400 Senior Thesis Class Notes,* 2014.

this passage literally! Recalling, 1 Corinthians 13:1-3 again. In this passage, Paul masterfully uses hyperbolic rhetoric to present himself as a personal example of this teaching in 1 Corinthians 13:1-3 (compare to 1 Corinthians 9).

b. *Repetition.* I often told my hermeneutics classes that repetition is God's megaphone and He is saying, "Pay attention." For example, in 1 Corinthians 1:18-31 we find the word "wisdom," its cognates (e.g., wise) and synonyms (discernment), are repeated thirteen (13) times. Obviously, Paul wants us to pay attention to this word and its various forms.

c. *Irony.* The storyteller of events in the book of Esther is quite a fan of using irony.[8] Perhaps, one of the most ironically comic scenes in the entire book of Esther is captured in Esther 6:1-13. Mordecai's foe, Haman, plots and makes plans for Mordecai's outrageous death; however, in the same scene the king plans to honor Mordecai's faithful service. Honestly, when I read Esther, I find myself laughing out loud at the futile attempts of Haman and others.

d. *Simile.* Authors use similes to make a direct comparison. Look for words such as "like" or "as" to signal evidence of a simile. The book of Malachi is rich in the use of similes. For example, *like* a refiner's fire (3:2b) and *like* fullers' soap (3:2b) are similes.

e. *Metaphor.* Like the simile, metaphors make a comparison, but unlike the simile, we will not find words "like" or "as" in metaphorical statements. Jesus used metaphors when He said, "you are the salt of the earth . . . you are the light of the world" (Matthew 5:13-14). David, a retired shepherd, used the metaphor of "Shepherd" for the Lord in the beloved Psalm 23.

f. *Word plays.* Nabal's name means fool, and guess what? He acted foolishly (see 1 Samuel 25). Also in Esther 1, the narrator uses a play on words to remind us of the Persians' heavy

8. Karen Jobes' *Commentary on the Book of Esther* is excellent and worthy of your purchase.

and extravagant drinking. That is, the original audience would have heard a rhyming between Vashti's name and the Hebrew words for *drinking* and *feast*.

g. *Euphemism.* Sometimes a harsh expression can be expressed more mildly, or indirectly . . . or in a less embarrassing way; this is a euphemism. For example, "falling asleep" is a euphemism for death; "to lay with" is an euphemism for sexual intercourse.

h. *Chiasmus.* A chiasmus, known as inverted parallelism, is used for stylistic purposes or for emphasis. A few examples include Isaiah 6:10, Mark 2:27, Esther 2:7 and James 3:1-4:12:

Isaiah 6:10

    [*A*] Heart

      [*B*] Ears

        [C] Eyes

        [C'] Eyes

      [*B'*] Ears

    [*A'*] Heart

Esther 2:7

    [*A*] Daughter of his uncle

      [*B*] Neither father nor mother

        [C] Beautiful figure and lovely to look at

      [*B'*] Father and mother died

    [*A'*] Mordecai take her as his own daughter

Mark 2:27

    [*A*] Sabbath

      [B] Man

      [B'] Man

    [*A'*] Sabbath

James 3:1–4:12

[A] Misuse of the tongue (3:1-12)

[B] Live by "wisdom from above" (3:13-18)

[A'] Misuse of the tongue (4:1-12)

A' is an inverted image of, and parallels, *A*; likewise *B'* is an inverted reflection of, and parallels, *B*. As you can see, authors use a chiasmus to draw our attention to their *main idea*: eyes, man, Esther's beautiful figure and lovely appearance, and live by "wisdom from above."

i. *Inclusio.* An author uses an inclusio to "box" in or frame a piece of literature. For example, compare Matthew 4:23 and Matthew 9:35. We have nearly the same rendition: "And Jesus went throughout all the cities and villages, *teaching* in their synagogues and *proclaiming* the gospel of the kingdom and *healing* every disease and every affliction." This is the author's way of saying that the verses sandwiched between these two bookends provide concrete illustrations of Jesus' teaching, proclaiming, and healing ministry.

j. *Questions.* Questions in the Bible typically come in two varieties: real questions and rhetorical questions. Rhetorical questions "which constitute 70 percent found in the New Testament,"[9] are indirect, and tend to be used by the speaker to engage the audience in a "think and respond" fashion. For example, in James 2:14, James asks, "What good is it, my brothers, if someone says he has faith but does not have works? He expects his audience to think and respond (silently), "Not good." Direct questions are that—they are asked directly and seek a direct answer. For example, when Peter ended his impromptu preaching on the Day of Pentecost, people asked a direct question, "What must I do to be saved?"

k. *Idioms.* "It cost me an arm and a leg." "You cannot judge a book by its cover." "It's raining cats and dogs." "It cost me

9. Beekman and Callow, *Translating the Word of God*, 229.

some blood, sweat, and tears." "The glass is half-full" or "I am tied up this weekend." What do all these phrases have in common? They are figurative, and not to be taken literally; and many of these particular idioms are indigenous; namely, they have likely originated in America. And the meaning of most of these idioms is known to us, or at the very least, we know when to use them. Idioms are common in the Bible too. And, like American idioms, they are figurative and indigenous. Uncovering the meaning of Biblical idioms is *par for the course* for understanding passages of Scripture. For example, in 2 Samuel 18:25 a messenger is recorded as having "good news in his mouth," which means to bring good news. In Luke 13:32 King Jesus calls King Herod a "fox," which means he was "weak" and/or "unclean."

l. *Numeric literary device.* Proverbs 6:16–19 is an interesting passage. Yet, we need to ask—"what is the context?" Many times we take the verses in the book of Proverbs separately without taking the surrounding verses into consideration; that is, we disregard the literary context. Surprisingly, many of the Proverbs are couched in a context, or rather, are part of a unit (e.g. Proverbs 16:1–9). Similarly, Proverbs 6:16–19 is part of a larger literary unit; namely, Proverbs 6:12–19. In this unit, the author describes a person who seeks to cause strife among others. The author uses two representative descriptions: 1) characteristics of a worthless person (vv. 12–15) and 2) things that the Lord hates (vv. 16–19). The author uses a numeric literary device to highlight a representative list of sins that the Lord hates, for the sole purpose of shining a spotlight on the easy-to-overlook, seventh sin: "a false witness who breathes out lies." Psalm 101:3–7 employs a similar numeric literary convention.[10]

---

10. Kselman,, "Psalm 101," 45–62.

Word Studies

The purpose of a word study is to determine whether a word has a range of meanings, and if so, which meaning an author intended in a given context. Word studies can also reveal nuances of meaning that may not be clear in translation. Initially, we ask: has the literary context analysis defined key terms in our passage of Scripture? If not, we might need to do a "word study." Here are few instances where a word study paid off:

- *Hate.* Understanding the various meanings of the word 'hate' is vital to understanding Malachi 1:1-5. Malachi 1:2b-3 says, "Yet I have loved Jacob, but Esau I have *hated.*" This naturally rubs us the wrong the way, primarily because of this oft repeated cliché, "God hates the sin but loves the sinner." However, as Carson writes, "This cliché should be abandoned because fourteen times in the first fifty psalms alone, we are told that God hates the sinner, his wrath is on the liar, and so forth. In the Bible, the wrath of God rests both on sin (Romans 1:18–32) and on *the sinner* (John 3:36)."[11] Carson is right, God hates sinners—see Psalm 11:5—"the Lord hates the wicked—i.e., those among God's people who would exploit and harm others, and thereby foil the very purpose of the covenant, arouse God's anger, and render themselves liable to severe judgment (v. 6)."[12] See also Psalm 5:5 in which the psalmist declares that God "hates all evildoers." God hates because His divine justice demands such. The word, hate, in Malachi is the same word as used by the psalmists but with one important difference: the word hate in this Malachi passage is not of the emotionally charged variety. We need to consider the context of the entire Old Testament in covenantal terms. Again, while yet in Rebekah's womb, God *chose* Jacob but not Esau. That's the sense of the word here. In other words, "to hate" here means, "to not choose." Or we might think of 'hate' as Jesus uses the word in Luke 14:26. Here,

---

11. Carson, *The Difficult Doctrine of Love of God,* 68–69.

12. Dennis, et al., *ESV,* 952.

'hate,' is a Semitic expression meaning to love less (see Genesis 29:30-31; Deuteronomy 21:15-17; Matthew 10:37). God loved Esau less by not electing him. Because "Scripture interprets Scripture," this is the same sense of "hate" used by Jesus in Luke 14:26-27. Specifically, to "hate one's family" means that Christ should have our primary affection, all others including family has our secondary affection.

- *Mystery.* When we think of the word 'mystery', we often think words like "scary," "unknown," "secret" or something to be solved. When I think of the word, 'mystery' for instance, I think of the NBC Dateline's, "Real Life Mysteries" or I think of the many crime murder mystery TV shows. For the Greek, Hellenistic and Roman pagan mystery religions, a 'mystery' was secretly imparted knowledge and esoteric so that only a few initiated elite understood these 'mysteries'; however, Paul hijacked and emptied this word of the meaning known to these pagan cults and poured in a different meaning. So, for Paul, the word "mystery" in Colossians 1:24-2:5 is referring to mysteries freely and openly communicated to all. Namely, the truths once hidden are now revealed and accessible to all. Paul's letter to the Romans elaborates, "my gospel and the proclamation of Jesus Christ, according to the revelation of the mystery hidden for long ages past, but now revealed and made known through the prophetic writings by the command of the eternal God, so that all nations might believe and obey Him" (Romans 16:25-26). So, then this Christian mystery, is God's embracing purpose of redemption through Christ (Romans 16:25).[13]

What resources do you need to do a word study?

1. Bible Dictionary

2. Concordance

3. Several versions of the Bible—dynamic and formal equivalents

---

13. Douglas and Tenney, *Dictionary of the Bible*, 685.

4. Vine's Complete Expository Dictionary of Old and New Testament Words (optional but a good investment)

For more on how to choose a word to study and to see an example of an actual word study, see Appendix C.

Others Tools

There are other analysis tools for the aspiring layperson. They include the following:

a. *Old in the New.* What Old Testament Scriptures are quoted verbatim or alluded to in the New Testament passage of Scripture? For example, Matthew's account is replete with quoted Old Testament passages because he was trying to prove to a Jewish audience that Jesus was the fulfillment of many Old Testament Scriptures. What Old Testament practices and concepts are alluded to in the New Testament passage of Scripture? This reminds me of something I often told my students: the New Testament writers' Bible was the Old Testament. Jesus' Bible was the Old Testament. So, it behooves us, exegetes, to know the Old Testament Scriptures well!

b. *Dialogue or Discourse Analysis.* Discourse analysis is yet another interpretive tool to arrive at the meaning of a text. "A discourse can be a letter, a sermon, a public address, a conversation, or even a poem, a song, or a prayer, as long as it makes assertions."[14] A Biblical character's speech reveals much about the character (e.g. thoughts and motives) and dialogue advances the plot of the story. God and Abram carry on a conversation in Genesis 15, for example; most of Job is a dialogue between his uncompassionate friends and God. Keep in mind that studying the dialogue between the actors in the story affords us these benefits:

1. It is often in dialogue that we get a significant clue to the story plot and to the character of the speakers;

14. Doriani, *Getting the Message*, 78–79.

2. Dialogue, especially contrastive dialogue, affords further characterization clues; and;

3. Very often the narrator will emphasize the crucial parts of the narrative by having one of the characters repeat or summarize the narrative in a speech.

More about Genre Plus

The exegete can expect genres to behave a certain way. Remember, the function of a literary piece will not betray its genre (or form). Generally speaking, Biblical authors often do the following:

- Use elevated, or poetic diction, or speech to emphasize significance (e.g., Genesis 2:18-25). Genesis 1 is also an excellent example of exalted prose. Speaking of genre, Genesis 1:1-2:3 is a different genre than Genesis 2:4-25. In other words, a book can have multiple genres operating.

- Aim to give us more than simple facts; "they want to capture our imaginations, to enable our whole person to lean into life with a vigorous faith and a zeal for goodness."[15]

- Use divine action, symbolism, and imaginative elements. In other words, authors use images to help us picture something; so the images are about something real. For example, the serpent was told that "dust you shall eat all the days of your life" in Genesis 3:14. This image—"dust you shall eat all the days of your life"—describes the humiliation the serpent will experience *forever*.

- Use language that should be taken literally (e.g., "honor your father and mother") and figuratively (e.g., "if your eye causes you to sin, then pluck it out").

- Choose the appropriate genre to communicate God's thoughts.

15. Collins, *Did Adam and Eve Really Exist?*, 20.

At the end of the day the Biblical writers, under the guidance of the Holy Spirit, the Chief Superintendent, sought to craft their piece, so that "[it would be] useful for teaching, rebuking, correcting and training in righteousness, so that the servant of God may be thoroughly equipped for every good work" (2 Timothy 3:16–17).

Table 2. Exegete's Expectations
per Old Testament Genres

Genre	Expectations
Prose—includes Law, Narrative, History	*Laws*, while on the surface may appear dull; they provide a "radically different view of human community and the social values it promotes."[a] Old Testament laws must be understood against a covenantal backdrop: God rescues or redeems a people and enters into a covenant relationship with them. The laws, therefore, must be interpreted relationally. These laws governed Israel's relationship with our gracious God. While many of the laws are strange to us, they provide "timeless ethical, moral and theological principles."[b] The laws were not to be practiced to earn salvation; rather, the laws were to show the Israelites (and us) the character of God and our need for the Perfect Law Keeper, Jesus Christ. As the Perfect Law Keeper, the Laws show us what "Christ-likeness" looks like.

Genre	Expectations
	Narratives make up over 40% of the Old Testament.[c] Narratives simply recount the past. However, biblical writers never write or report everything as their purposes are to instruct rather than to inform; to teach us rather than spell out all the facts. Jobes' words emphasize this last point, "When reading 'history,' our taste for facts, and nothing but the facts, raises expectations that are sometimes disappointed by the ancient genres found in Scripture."[d] Narrators' emphasis, so then, will be on *showing* (displaying the heart by action and speech) versus *telling* (telling us explicitly what kind of person the character is). So, we must infer or read between the lines. For example, in the book of Ruth, we can infer that Ruth converted and placed her belief/trust in Yahweh (see Ruth 1:16). Look for seemingly insignificant details and ask why did the author mention that? For example, in Judges we find that Ehud was "left-handed"—why would the author mention this?

Genre	Expectations
	Biblical history, like all history, is a record or representation of the events. Historical accountings will be different. Remember that biblical writers never write or report everything; that is, they are intentionally selective in what they report. Nonetheless, Biblical history is the reporting of real events (important for the veracity of the Bible). Biblical history, like American history, will discuss places, people, and things. Biblical history will be artistic, entertaining, anthological, realistic, romantic, revelatory, response-evoking and among all else, theological.[e] Do not expect history to be told chronologically. Compare, for example, 1 Kings 14:19-20 and 1 Kings 15:1. Expect to infer principles; for example, in 2 Kings 4:1-7 we can infer this principle: God sometimes invites us to participate in our redemptive remedy.

Genre	Expectations
Prophecy -includes Major prophets (Isaiah, Jeremiah, Ezekiel, and Daniel) and the Twelve Minor Prophets	*Prophecy* captures prophets—God's covenant enforcers—both forth-telling and foretelling (i.e., making predictions about the future). Some-times these 'future events' were im-mediately fulfilled in the lifecycles of Israel, Judah or surrounding nations. Keep in mind what the prophets *did* is given more ink than what they *said*. Consider for example, Hosea. He is requested to marry Gomer who later cheats on him. Isaiah preaches naked (see Isaiah 20). And an Ethio-pian rescues Jeremiah (see Jeremiah 38). Keep in mind that most of the longer books—the Major Prophets—are a collection of spoken oracles not presented chronologically. Expect to labor in understanding the words spoken by the prophets because "as people far removed from the reli-gious, historical and cultural life of ancient Israel, we simply have great trouble putting the words spoken by the prophets in their original histori-cal context. [So] it is often hard for us to see what they are referring to and why."[f] Expect to see prophets channel their poetic side as well.

Genre	Expectations
Poetry -includes Psalms, Wisdom Literature	*Poetry* uses language that is highly metaphorical; the psalms capture "the emotions of each soul"[8]—from the depths of being betrayed by a close friend to the exhilaration of being rescued from a ruthless enemy. So, Hebrew poetry is addressed to the head through the heart. Expect to spend more time discovering the meaning behind the metaphorical language and images; and expect more effort required to situate the psalm in its historical context.
	Wisdom literature, such as the Proverbs, captures the application of wisdom to times not our own; this means that we must carefully evaluate if a pithy wisdom statement is applicable to our modern day situation. And if so, how? Expect wisdom literature to use contradictions—e.g., compare Proverbs 26:4 and Proverbs 26:5.

Table 3. Exegete's Expectations
per New Testament Genres

Genre	Expectations
Narrative -includes Gospels, Acts	The *Gospels* are the only four books in the Bible that convey the life and teachings of Jesus Christ. Although the Gospels have a genre parallel in the ancient world that was called the *bios,* do not expect the Gospels to follow the modern day criteria of a biography—which is typically a written chronical account of someone's life that includes perhaps a discussion of the person's physical description, psychological thinking, and/ or personal development. "Rather than focusing on physical description and psychological thinking and personal development like modern biographies, a '*bios*' highlighted the key events that surrounded a person and his teaching."[h] Expect to "see" a good portion of the Gospel account according to Mark contents in the Gospels according to Matthew and Luke as all three are considered "synoptic gospels" where synoptic means "seeing with the same eye."

Genre	Expectations
	The ***Acts of the Apostles*** is considered the history of the first church and is the sequel to the Gospel of Luke. As history this book features two main figures: Peter, the apostle to the Jews, and Paul, the apostle to the Gentiles. As history (and unlike the gospels), expect a chronological accounting of history. And like all narratives, author and historian, Luke was selective in what he chose to report.

Genre	Expectations
Epistolary Literature—includes Paul's Letters and the General Epistles like Hebrews, James, 1, 2 Peter, 1, 2, 3 John	***Paul's letters*** typically address an issue or several issues. And in light of these issues, these letters capture the working out of Christ's teaching in regards to beliefs and conduct of emerging Christian communities with, of course, application to our communities. Some principles from Paul's letters will be universal; other principles must be drawn from practices unique to Paul's time. For example, greeting someone of the same-sex with a kiss on the cheek was a common practice in Paul's day; the application—greet each other warmly. Look for this pattern in the Pauline epistles: a discussion of what God has done in Christ (known as the 'indicative') followed by a discussion of what we should do in response (known as the "imperative") ***Hebrews and the General Epistles*** vary from what we expect to find in epistles—like an opening greeting or salutation and closing; for example, the book of Hebrews does not begin like a letter—there is no salutation. The book of Hebrews is a written sermon. James' epistle stresses three major themes: trials and temptations, wisdom and speech, and wealth and poverty.[i]

Genre	Expectations
Apocalyptic Literature -includes Revelation	Expect the book of ***Revelation*** to simultaneously expose and hide its messages with both rich symbolic imagery and language that is ambiguous. It is okay for the exegete to say, "its meaning is not entirely clear." The exegete is encouraged "to study each scene and each image in light of what Revelation itself tells about them, in light of relevant Old Testament backgrounds, and in view of other historical information of which John's first-century audience would have been aware."[j]

a. Klein, et al., Introduction to Biblical Interpretation, 341.

b. Ibid., 345.

c. Fee and Stuart, How to Read the Bible, 120.

d. Jobes, Esther, 32.

e. Adapted from David Howard's "An Introduction to the Old Testament Historical Books," 44–49.

f. Fee and Stuart, How to Read the Bible, 190.

g. Saint Patriarch, Athanasius on the Psalms, 47.

h. Dennis, L. T. et al., ESV Bible, 1811.

i. Klein, et al., Introduction to Biblical Interpretation, 433.

j. Ibid., 445.

Conclusion

The Bible writers employed a vast array of genres to imaginatively and wonderfully recount God's story. However, keep in mind that sometimes poetry is embedded in prophecy; sometimes poetry, such as songs, are embedded in epistles (for example, Colossians 1:15–20 is thought to be an early hymn of the church[16]); and sometimes poetry is embedded in narratives (see Mary's Song in Luke 2:46–55). Nevertheless, the behavior and expectations of a piece of literature will align closely with its literary type or genre. Paying attention to the genre is one of those safeguards that the Holy Spirit puts in place to help us manage our expectations, and to help us discipline ourselves so that we do not impose the behavior of one genre onto another. Respect and embrace genre analysis. Likewise, be on the lookout for words to study in a bit more detail, the occurrences of Old Testament passages quoted verbatim or alluded to in the New Testament, and lastly, discourse analysis is a necessary step when the genre type is narrative.

16. Liderbach, *Christ in the Early Christian Hymns*, 47.

5

Redemptive Remedy

"[Our] Holy God is redemptive, not abandoning."[1]

—Rosaria Champagne Butterfield

Reality Check: Living In Post Genesis 3

WE LIVE IN A post Genesis 3 world. The events of Genesis 3 were a game-changer for humanity. In Genesis 3, the Serpent's line of questioning planted doubt in Eve's mind that God was selfishly withholding something, and thus, could not be trusted! Eve, in defiance of God's commandment to not eat from the tree of knowing good and evil, took fruit from this tree, and shared it with Adam, her husband, thereby implicating him, too, in this treasonous crime! The "rest" they say, "is history." We do not have to look very far to see evidence of our first parents' historical fall from grace, known as the Fall of Man. We do not have to look very far, because every person has inherited Adam's sinful nature. An octopus extends his reach because of his tentacles. Similarly, the sin "parasite"[2] has several tentacles and these tentacles have aggressively touched or invaded every millimeter of our body. Because of this harsh reality, we can ask any passage of Scripture these two questions:

---

1. Butterfield, *The Secret Thoughts*, 47.
2. Plantinga, *A Breviary of Sin*, 89.

1. What aspect of the human condition is revealed in this passage?

2. What is God's gracious remedy for *this* human condition?

As fallen people, the range of human conditions that the Bible addresses is as wide "as the curse is found,"[3] because the Bible features broken people like us! For example, here's *a condensed list* of the human conditions that the Bible addresses . . . and most importantly, where God meets us with a redemptive remedy:

✓ Fear

✓ Anxiety

✓ Perverted ideas about sex and sexuality

✓ Being presumptuous

✓ Lack of assurance

✓ Selfishness

✓ Entertaining evil thoughts

✓ Idolatry

✓ Laziness

✓ Stealing

✓ Discriminating, showing partiality

✓ Coveting what belongs to others

✓ Divided heart

✓ Envy, jealously

✓ Disrespecting those in authority

✓ Discontentment

✓ Infertility

✓ Abandonment, betrayal

✓ Disrespecting those in authority

✓ Improper worship

✓ Fornication

✓ Failing to parent one's children

✓ Incestuous actions and thoughts

✓ Spiritual blindness

✓ Greed

✓ Slander, lying, quarreling, etc.

✓ Worry

✓ Pride

✓ Disbelief

✓ Adultery, adulterous thoughts

✓ Gluttony

✓ Hypocrisy

✓ Neglecting matters of social justice

✓ And many more

---

3. See Michael Williams' wonderfully written book, "As Far As the Curse is Found."

Of course, the number of human conditions that the Bible addresses is plentiful; however, the good news is that "[our] Holy God is redemptive, not abandoning."[4] Our gracious God is eager to administer His redemptive remedy. Let's test this notion.

The English Standard Version (ESV) of the Bible records Genesis 11:1–9 (ESV) as follows:

> 1 Now the whole earth had one language and the same words. 2 And as people migrated from the east, they found a plain in the land of Shinar and settled there. 3 And they said to one another, "Come, let us make bricks, and burn them thoroughly." And they had brick for stone, and bitumen for mortar. 4 Then they said, "Come, let us build ourselves a city and a tower with its top in the heavens, and let us make a name for ourselves, lest we be dispersed over the face of the whole earth." 5 And the Lord came down to see the city and the tower, which the children of man had built. 6 And the Lord said, "Behold, they are one people, and they have all one language, and this is only the beginning of what they will do. And nothing that they propose to do will now be impossible for them. 7 Come, let us go down and there confuse their language, so that they may not understand one another's speech." 8 So the Lord dispersed them from there over the face of all the earth, and they left off building the city. 9 Therefore its name was called Babel, because there the Lord confused the language of all the earth. And from there the Lord dispersed them over the face of all the earth.

Thus far, we have studied S, C and A of the acronym *SCAR*; this chapter completes our acronym as we discuss "R"; where "R" stands for the Redemptive Remedy. One may ask, "Where is the redemption in Genesis 11:1–9?" Or better, we might say, "God is the Hero of every passage of Scripture; so from what (or who) do His people need rescuing?"

Before we answer this question, let's define 'redemption.' Often when we think of 'redemption,' most of us think of Christ and

---

4. Butterfield, *The Secret Thoughts*, 47.

His finished work on our behalf; of course, this is true, however, this is much too narrow, as well. In other words, the word *redemption* has such a wide semantic range of meanings, including:

- God reconciling two warring factions
- God's salvation
- God's inflicting harm on our enemies on our behalf
- God's exonerating us from a wrongful accusation
- God's fighting for His people—God fought on behalf of His people to slay the taunting Goliath; yes, God used David; however, *God did* the heavy lifting redemptive work. God is the hero of this passage!
- God's gracious pursuit of sinners—God, in the person of Jesus Christ, pursued the Samaritan Woman in John 4; He pursued the church ravishing Saul; and He pursued Zacchaeus in Luke 19:1–10. And God graciously pursued (and continues to pursue) us.
- God's laws—God's laws are concerned with the preserving of life and this echoes the character of a life-giving, life-preserving Lord.
- God's restoration of something that was previously lost—in Matthew 6, God assures those who have lost confidence in God's provisions and are prone to be anxious that God cares for the birds of the air and how much more for us when He provides our needs. Psalm 23 is a song of confidence in God's ongoing care and as such it serves to restore our hope.

Here's the main point—at the conclusion of doing *SCAR*, I:

- Should have a feel and familiarity for the passage of Scripture;
- Should know the literary and cultural-historical contexts and the benefits that afford me to understand the passage of Scripture;
- Should have gained additional insight into our passage of Scripture after doing a thorough analysis;

- Should be able to confidently answer these two overarching interpretative questions:

    1. What aspect of the human condition is revealed in this passage?

    2. What is God's gracious remedy for *this* human condition?

Note, if you are not able to answer these two questions confidently, review your notes, review any unanswered questions, practice humility and ask someone who will be honest with you (see HP#9), etc.

So, back to my initial question—what is God's redemptive remedy in the passage above, Genesis 11:1-9? Let's take a closer look . . . or explore together . . . .

First some *context*—God mandated our first parents, Adam and Eve, in Genesis 1:26-28 to be fruitful and multiply and to fill the earth. Implied here is that Adam and Eve (and their descendants) were to reproduce and move out from Eden to "fill the earth." Through this narrative, however, we learn that instead of filling the earth, Adam's descendants "migrated from the east" and decided to *congregate* in one place, the land of Shinar (see vs. 2). You might be asking, "What's the foul here?" The foul is that this coming together is contrary to what God mandated Adam (and by inference, his descendants) to do in Genesis 1:26–28. This is the first issue.

The second foul is that in their collective hubris these people thought that they could build a temple-tower structure to top the heavens—God's throne room or dwelling place. These rebels did not want to build a tower to get closer, and more intimate, with God; rather, these rebels wanted to build a temple-tower, a symbol of human autonomy, to "make a name for themselves" (vs. 4). In essence, they wanted the notoriety and fame of a celebrity. However, God had seen, and had enough, and He saw this as a slippery slope. If these people achieve this feat, Moses writes, "this is only the beginning of what they will [conjure up in their minds and] do"[5] (vs. 6). In other words, God was concerned that this act of arrogance would lead to more acts of arrogance. God comes down and confuses their language (vs. 7). Do you see the irony here? God has to come down to see His people's feeble attempts to build a tower to reach the heavens. It is laughable that God *comes down* to this what had to be an itty-bitty construction effort.

Again, where is the redemption in this passage? God redeems this situation, one, by saving these people from themselves—by confusing their language God prevents them from getting into more collective mischief; and two, He saves them by confusing their one common language which essentially causes them to disperse (which was God's original desire in Genesis 1:26-28); they disperse because they could not understand each other. We might say God restores His original plan by confusing this people's language.[6]

Meaning of this Passage of Scripture: At the Intersection of Two Answers

What aspect of the human condition is revealed in this passage? *Mankind's natural bent to disobey and proclivity to be arrogant.*

What is God's gracious remedy for *this* human condition? *God scatters the people so that they will not conspire and get into more sin.*

So, as was mentioned in Chapter 2, the intersection of these two answers reveals the original meaning of this passage of Scripture as: God often will intervene to protect us from our sinful behaviors.

---

5. God redeems our first parents' transgression by kicking them out of the garden. In other words, their expulsion from the garden is an act of mercy as God did not want to see Adam and Eve's rebellious state exacerbated "lest they reach out his hand and take also from the tree of life and eat, and live forever" (see Genesis 3:22-23).

6. The discerning reader will see that Genesis 11:1-9 provides the "genesis" or birth of the nations in Genesis 10:1-32. Again, the literary context—reading what comes before and after Genesis 11:1-9 provides that insight.

Part 2

Pulling It All Together

6

Pulling it All Together:
Applying *SCAR* to
Old Testament Passages

Now that I have shared the Hermeneutical Principles (HPs) to interpret by and have introduced you to *SCAR*, it is time to *pull it all together* and *SCAR* some actual passages of Scripture. This chapter applies *SCAR* to *two* Old Testament passages: Genesis 15:1–21 and Psalm 23. And in the next chapter, Chapter 7, I *SCAR* two New Testament passages. Located in Appendix E, I list the Hermeneutical principles (HPs) and summarize *SCAR* for you; use this as a 'cheat sheet'.

HP#1 reminds us that "The Holy Spirit is our chief superintendent when doing biblical interpretation" . . . so, I offer this brief prayer: "Lord, Holy Spirit, open wide our eyes that we might behold wonderful things from your Word."

SCAR Genesis 15:1–21

[S]CAR—*Sit* awhile with this passage and make a list of questions you have. Compare your list with my list below.

1. What is a vision? And how do words come to person via a vision? (vs. 1) Did God and Abram have a conversation like a two human beings conversing? Is this the first time God and Abram spoke?

2. What does it mean to say, "the word of the Lord came"? (vs. 1)

3. Who is Abram? (vs. 1)

4. Why did God greet Abram with "fear not"? (vs. 1)

5. What does it mean when God says, "I am your shield"? (vs. 1)

6. What is the nature of this "reward"? (vs 1)

7. What is an heir? And who is Eliezer of Damascus? (vs. 2)

8. God promises Abram his "very own son"—does this come to pass? (vs. 4)

9. God promises many offspring to Abram—does this come to pass? (vs. 5)

10. What does it mean for Abram to "believe the Lord"? And what does it mean for the Lord to count it to him as righteousness? (vs. 6)

11. Where is Ur of the Chaldeans? (vs. 7)

12. What 'land' was God referring to? (vv. 7, 13 and 18)

13. Is there any significance for God to request these specifically aged animals—a heifer *three* years old and a female goat *three* years old? And why did God request Abram bring two birds—a turtledove and a young pigeon? (vs. 9)

14. Why did Abram cut these animals in half and lay each half over against the other? But Abram did not cut the birds in half—why? (vs. 10)

15. What does it mean for a "deep sleep" to befall Abram? Did God administer anesthesia? (vs. 12)

16. Who are these "sojourners"? And in what land will they dwell and be afflicted for 400 years? (vs. 13)

17. God brings judgment on this nation where Abram's offspring will dwell—what is the nature of this judgment? (vs. 14)

18. God promises that Abram will go to his fathers in peace—did this come to pass? (vs. 15)

19. Did Abram's offspring return to this land in the fourth generation? (vs. 16)

20. What does "the iniquity of the Amorites is not yet complete" mean? (vs. 16)

21. A smoking fire pot and a flaming torch passed between the pieces that Abram had cut in half—what does this ceremony mean? (vs. 17)

22. What does it mean when God says, "the Lord made a covenant with Abram?" (vs. 18)

23. What relationship does making the covenant have with God's statement, "to your offspring I give this land . . . ?" (vs. 18)

24. Where is this land described to Abram in vv. 18–21?

S[C]AR

Here we again consider two contexts discussed in Chapter 3: literary and the cultural-historical contexts.

The Literary Context

Remember two things: one, at this point in the process we rely on our study of the Bible solely (*no* resources are consulted at this point); and two, the literary context analyzes passages just *before* and *after* our passage of Scripture.

In this case, the literary context of Genesis 15 is quite wide, as the literary context is bracketed by Genesis 11:10–14:24 and Genesis 16:1–25:18. Here is a "rough" top-level outline:[1]

---

1. Outlining is a wonderful tool to pictorially illustrate the literary context.

"The Call and Commissioning of Abraham and his spiritual development"

- Genesis 11:11–26: Abram a descendent of Shem

- Genesis 11:27–32: Terah (Abram's Father) Moves the Family: Ur of the Chaldeans to Haran

- Genesis 12:1–3: Abram, the "new Adam," [2] called and commissioned to be the conduit of blessing to all the families[3] of the earth; God makes promises

- Genesis 12:4–9: Abram and nephew Lot depart from Haran

- Genesis 12:10–20: Abram's first lie

- Genesis 13–14: Abram and Lot separate; God reassures Abram of land and offspring

- Genesis 14: Abram rescues Lot; Melchizedek blesses Abram

- *[Genesis 15:1–21: God reassures Abram of Land and Offspring Again with an Extraordinary Act]*

- Genesis 16:1–16: Abram and Sarai are impatient

- Genesis 17:1–18:21: Name changes, Covenant of Circumcision enacted and Promise of Isaac's birth

- Genesis 18:22–33: Abraham prays on behalf of Sodom and Gomorrah

- Genesis 19:1–38: Sodom and Gomorrah destroyed, God rescues Lot

- Genesis 20:1–18: Abraham's second lie

- Genesis 21:1–34: Isaac's birth, God protects Hagar and Ishmael

- Genesis 22:1–24: God tests Abraham's obedience

---

2. This was God's original intent for Adam to be a righteous blessing to the people spread over the earth.

3. The families (or nations) created after God confuses the people's language (see Genesis 10–11).

- Genesis 23:1–20: Death and burial of Sarah

- Genesis 24:1–67: Isaac, Rebekah and Laban

- Genesis 25:1–18: Abraham remarries and his death

Notice that all these passages concern Abram (or his immediate family). This literary context analysis tells us the following:

- God has broached topics such as Abram's childlessness[4], the promise of innumerable offspring, and the promise of land before. The promise of innumerable offspring appears in Genesis 13:14–17 and 22:17, and the promise of land is front-and-center in Genesis 12:7. In fact, we find nearly the exact language, "to your offspring I will give this land,"[5] as we find in Genesis 15:18. God's promise of making him into a "great nation" in Genesis 12:2 implies the promise of land, and people, because the anatomy of a nation includes four constituent parts: a leader, *land*, a law/constitution, and *people*.

- And, if we travel back to Genesis 2:18–25, we will see that Abram was not the only person to experience a "deep sleep" because Adam was the first to undergo a deep sleep (Genesis 2:21). However, we must ask, is "deep sleep" being used in the same fashion in our passage. In other words, this might be a case where "Scripture interprets Scripture." We are first introduced to the river Euphrates in Genesis 2:14.

- With the words, "after these things," we are given a clue that this is a new revelation.

Self-Contained Passage

By doing this literary context analysis, it is clear that Genesis 15:1-21 is indeed a unit of Scripture. This is passage about God interfacing

---

4. Abram and Sarai's childlessness cited as early as Genesis 11:30.
5. The promise of land echoes "to give you this land" in Leviticus 25:38.

with one character only: Abram, and this passage fits nicely in the progression of Abram's story from Genesis 11 to Genesis 25.

The Cultural-Historical Context

Our cultural-historical context analysis considers life in this ancient society. Among the things we consider here are geography, modes of travel, rituals, customs, societal structure, dress, architecture, agriculture, family structure, and climate. We also ask about what was happening economically, militarily, politically, religiously, and philosophically. We need resources at this juncture so reaching for resources at this point, like a Bible commentary and/or Study Bible, is allowed.

1. *Ritualistically*, after reading this passage of Scripture, the word "ritual" does not appear in this passage, but what is obvious is that Abram and God participated in a mysterious ritual. Remember that Abram has collected some animals and has cut them in half with the exception of the birds. He lays the carcass halves opposite each other, thus creating a bloody path. In ancient times, as Jeremiah 34:18 suggests, people entering a covenant would pass between the dismembered animals. This action of passing along this bloody path was interpreted as an enacted curse so if either party reneged on the stipulations of the covenant he would suffer the fate of the dismembered animals. However, notice something very striking from our passage: only God, His presence being represented as the smoking firepot and flaming torch, "walks the path." Do you get it? God is saying if I don't follow through on the promises of this covenant—land and offspring—I will invoke this curse on myself.

2. *Religiously*, Abram grew up in a context where several gods were served (see Joshua 24:1–2). Abram was known to be a henotheist—someone who believes in one God without

denying the existence of other gods.[6] So, interacting with a singular God like Yahweh must have been strange.

3. *Geographically*, this scene takes place in the future Promised Land (see Question #12 above). At the end of this narrative, God assures Abram that his descendants will occupy the same land where he has currently pitched his tent.

SC[A]R

Because we are dealing with a literary piece, let's answer these preliminary analytical questions:

- *Who is the author of Genesis?* And has this author contributed other works to the Bible? Moses is the author and he is credited with writing Leviticus, Numbers, Deuteronomy, and Exodus.

- *Who is the original audience?* The original audience are those who came out of Egypt.

- *Why is this book in the Bible?* The book of Genesis provides not only an exalted view of God as Creator and Sovereign King, but it also provides an early history of the Jewish nation.

- *What is the genre of this literary piece?* The genre is narrative; specifically narrative history, and it follows the topography of the curve in Figure 11 in Chapter 4, Analysis. This figure is repeated below for your convenience and consideration. Specifically, this narrative may be dissected as depicted in Table 4.

---

6. Williams, *Covenant Theology Class Notes.*

Table 4. Narrative Dissected by Stage

Stage in Story	Action
Opening scene	'A word for the Lord' comes to Abram in a vision: God's reassures Abram using military language (e.g., I am your shield or protector) (vs. 1)
Crisis	Abram, impassioned and exasperated, complains about still being childless; 'scene change'—Abram asked to leave tent and to come outside; and Abram believes Yahweh (vv. 2-6)
Climax	Abram's dismemberment of animals creates a bloody pathway; a deep sleep befalls Abram, more words of reassurance from God (vv. 7-16)
Denouement (or finale)	God vows a curse-oath to make good on His covenant promises of an offspring and land (vv. 17-21)

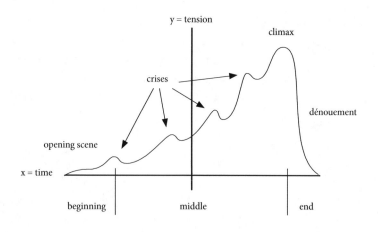

Dialogue Analysis: God and Abram Discuss

God opens the initial scene by uttering these words to Abram, "Do not fear, Abram, I am a shield to you; your reward shall be very great." With these words, we are introduced to Abram's human need. Consider what the literary context has told us: Abram has been told that from him a great nation will arise and that innumerable descendants will come from him; yet, *not one* descendant has been reproduced. Anxiety about the future and God's delay in fulfilling His promises has beset Abram. Thus, God speaks a word of comforting assurance: "fear not, I am your shield (or protection), *your very great reward*." Abram tries to "connect the dots" between his childlessness and God's statement of "your very great reward," but cannot.

Not convinced, Abram, in what appears to be an incredulous and accusatory tone, responds, back at God, "Sovereign Lord, what can you give me, since I remain childless and the one who will inherit my estate is Eliezer of Damascus?" And Abram said, "You have given me no children; so a servant in my household will be my heir" (Genesis 15:2–3, NIV). Abram's line of questioning expresses his main complaint against God: God's delay in fulfilling His promises. God knows Abram needs assurance so He responds "this man (Eliezer) will not be your heir; your very own son shall be your heir." And in a scene reminiscent of Genesis 13:14–17, God brings Abram out of his tent to gaze at heaven, and reassures him that his offspring will number the stars in heaven. However, Abram's fear is not allayed as he asks in vs. 8, "Sovereign Lord, how can I know that I will gain possession of it [the land]?"

As mentioned before, God's next words to Abram further the plot, "Bring me a heifer three years old, a female goat three years old, a ram three years old, a turtledove and a young pigeon" (vs. 9). We can infer that Abram knew what to do with the animals (as vs. 10 indicates). After God gives Abram a preview of the future (vv. 12–17), He again assures Abram of His promise to give his descendants the *land,* not with words, but rather with a meaningful ritual (vs. 17). Moses, the narrator, proves that this ritual was meant to assure Abram that his descendants will indeed possess this *land*, "On that day the Lord made a covenant with Abram and said, "To your descendants I give this *land*, from the river of Egypt to the great river, the Euphrates—the *land* of the Kenites, Kenizzites, Kadmonites, Hittites, Perizzites, Rephaites, Amorites, Canaanites, Girgashites and Jebusites" (vv. 18–21).

There are additional puzzles to solve at this analysis stage: namely, how do we define the word "vision," and as we discovered earlier, we need to define a few phrases in our passage. Below we solve these puzzles by answering some questions raised during the *sitting* stage of *SCAR*.

Questions and Answers

Question #1

Recall during the "Sitting" stage we asked the question, what is a vision and how do words come to person via a vision? Compare my notes with your own.

Source	Homework results
Word Biblical Commentary	The word used for 'vision' in this passage is rarely used in Hebrew; visions were a "recognized and very ancient mode of revelation."[a]
English Standard Version, Study Bible	"In a vision. Although it is not certain, the initial vision may have taken place at night"[b] as God brings Abram outside to count the stars.

Source	Homework results
The New International Dictionary of the Bible	"It is impossible to draw a sharp line of demarcation between dreams and visions. The Hebrew and Greek words all have to do with seeing. Visions in the Bible were for the most part given to individuals and *were not* apprehended by their companions. Through them God revealed to the seers truth in pictorial form."[c]

a. Wenham, Genesis 1:15, 327.

b. Dennis et al., ESV, 77.

c. Douglas and. Tenney, Bible Dictionary, 1052.

What can we deduce from this word study? A vision was a means for God to reveal a message to an audience of one: in this case, Abram. Keil and Delitzsch add this insightful explanation—this vision was, "an inward spiritual intuition and that not in a nocturnal vision, as in [Genesis] 46:2,"[7] but rather it occurred "in the day-time." And furthermore, this vision applies to the entire chapter; nowhere do we see a pause in the action or that the vision ceased before we get to the end of the chapter.

Other questions and answers:

Question #2: [vs. 1] "The word of the Lord came"—this phrase is typical of a prophet who introduces a revelation (see 1 Samuel 15:10; Hosea 1:1).

Question #4: [vs. 1] "I am your shield"—using military language, God promise to protect Abram.

7. Keil and Delitzsch, *Biblical Commentary*, 134.

Question #6: [vs. 1] "[I am] your reward"—God stands ready to richly reward Abram's confidence or ready obedience.

Question #9: [vs. 6] "He believed God and God created to him as righteousness"—in response to God's reassurance, Abram believed or trusted God—he became a believer in Yahweh—and God regarded Abram as now righteous.

Question #15: [vs. 12] "A deep sleep fell on Abram"—a "deep sleep that is preparatory for meeting God."[8]

Question #20: [vs. 16] "the iniquity of the Amorites is not yet complete"—as representing all the inhabitants of Canaan (the future promised land of Abram's descendants, the Israelites), the Amorites will experience God's judgment after they have become sufficiently wicked to deserve such a fate.

SCA**[R]**

Upon arrival to "R"—the Redemptive Remedy, we should also be able to confidently answer these two overarching questions:

1. What aspect of the human condition is revealed in this passage?

2. What is God's gracious remedy for *this* human condition?

What aspect of the human condition is revealed in this passage? Abram's anxiety and fear regarding God's timetable to fulfill His promises—of an offspring and of possessing land.

What is God's gracious remedy for *this* human condition? God assures Abram, with His words, about an offspring in vv. 4-5. And in a striking ritual, God assures Abram that his descendants will possess the land by taking a self-cursed oath.

---

8. Cotter, *Genesis*, 101.

Meaning of this Passage of Scripture: At the Intersection of Two Answers

The meaning of this short story can be found at the intersection of the answers to these two questions: What aspect of the human condition is revealed in this passage? And what is God's gracious remedy for *this* human condition? This short story, therefore, informs us that God is ready to reassure us in times of anxiety, fear, and uncertainty. Abram was fearful, exasperated over not having a child; but God reassures Abram that He will indeed deliver on His word because God is trustworthy.

SCAR Psalm 23

HP#1 reminds us that "The Holy Spirit is our chief superintendent when doing biblical interpretation" . . . so, I offer this brief prayer: "Lord, Holy Spirit, open wide our eyes that we might behold wonderful things from your Word."

[S]CAR

Sitting awhile with this beloved passage resulted in these questions. (Again, I invite you to do this exercise too and compare your list of questions.)

1. How is the Lord David's shepherd? Is David the only one to refer to God as his shepherd?

2. What does it mean to "shall not want"?

3. What is being conveyed by vs. 2, "He makes me lie down in green pastures . . . He leads me besides still waters"?

4. What does it mean to "restore my soul"? And why does my "soul need restoring"?

5. What is meant by vs. 3, "He leads me in paths of righteousness for His name's sake"?

6. Where is this "valley of the shadow of death"? Will I actually have to "walk through" this valley?

7. Is there some relationship between "I will fear no evil" and this valley of the shadow of death?

8. How is God with me? (vs. 4)

9. What is the purpose for a rod and staff and how do they comfort me?

10. What does it mean that God prepares a table before me in the presence of my enemies? Who are my enemies?

11. Was anointing someone's head with oil significant?

12. What does it mean that my "cup overflows"?

13. Will "goodness and mercy" actually trail me all the days of my earthly life or into eternity?

14. What does it mean to "dwell in the house of the Lord forever"? Is the "house of the Lord" the same as my local church?

S[C]AR

Literary Context

The book of Psalms is comprised of many individual units or self-contained passages of Scripture. However, it is still, nonetheless, a good practice to read the psalms that encircle our psalm, or Psalms 22 and 24. After reading Psalms 22 and 24 we discover that they offer us no assistance in interpreting our psalm; but this is not a futile exercise, as Psalms 22 and 24 are rich in theology and devotional material too. Keep in mind, however, that sometimes reading the psalm that comes before and after our psalm will pay handsome dividends. For example, while Psalm 42 and 43 are to be taken separately they, nonetheless, go well together. Likewise, Psalms 20–21 form a pair of royal psalms. The bottom-line: continue to practice the habit of reading the psalm immediately before the psalm being interpreted and the psalm immediately after your psalm.

Self-Contained Passage

This is a self-contained passage of Scripture because of two main reasons: 1) the psalmist begins and ends of a note of confidence (see vv. 1, 6) and 2) the psalmist provides why we should have confidence in God's care by using two different metaphors—as our shepherd and as our dinner host.

Cultural-Historical Context

Our cultural-historical context analysis considers life in this ancient society. Among the things we consider here are geography, modes of travel, rituals, customs, societal structure, dress, architecture, agriculture, family structure, and climate. We also ask about what was happening economically, militarily, politically, religiously, and philosophically. We need resources at this juncture so reaching for resources at this point, like a Bible commentary and/or Study Bible, is allowed.

Here we ask several questions to understand the cultural-historical context of our psalm:

1. *Historically and politically*, what was happening, or what had happened, to prompt David to pen this psalm? Historical and political questions are difficult to answer confidently. On one hand, Keil and Delitzch declare that "this Psalm belongs to the time of the rebellion under Absalom,"[9] while on the other hand, several commentaries[10] make no attempt to mention anything about historical or political context. One commentary dismisses the idea that this psalm was written against a particular historical or political backdrop and simply suggests that this psalm is David's "recollections on his own pastoral experience, although probably composed at a much later date."[11]

---

9. Keil and Delitzch, *Biblical Commentary*, 207.

10. These include commentaries such as Word Bible Commentary and Psalm 1–72 Tyndale Old Testament Commentary.

11. J. A. Alexander, *The Psalms—Translated & Explained*, (p. 107) and Bratcher and Reyburn, *A Handbook on the Psalms*, follow this line of reasoning.

2. *Custom-wise*, what does it mean to anoint someone's head with oil? The ancient custom of anointing someone's head, presumably with olive oil, was to communicate: you are a special guest. This explains Jesus' consternation with Simon who failed to anoint His head in Luke 7:46. Have I mentioned, before that a good exegete reads God's Word? The Holy Spirit will help you recall passages you have read when interpreting a passage of Scripture. I guarantee that!

3. *Geographically*, where could a shepherd locate "green pastures" or "still waters"? And geographically, where is this "valley of the shadow of death"? Or is the "valley of the shadow of death" to be taken metaphorically? What is meant by the "valley of the shadow of death"? With this phrase "the valley of the shadow of death," David, our poet, uses the most vivid and profound phrase here—this phrase for sheep meant a place that was ominous, dark as night, and dangerous at every turn. So, the poet, David, uses this phrase metaphorically.

4. *Vocationally*, what do we know of the shepherding occupation? And what do we know of sheep?

   a. Keep in mind that metaphors do break down eventually so we cannot press them too far; however, Bible writers when they use metaphors do us a favor—as it is from metaphors that we develop rich, robust, and sound theology. So, to say "Lord is Shepherd" is to say a lot, because it is considered a comprehensive metaphor. And we can surmise this by looking at the shepherd's job descripton. A shepherd in antiquity:

      i. Slept with his sheep to protect them from predators (e.g., bears, wolves, lions, etc.);

      ii. Gave his sheep names;

      iii. Served as his sheep's doctor—as the sheep were corralled into the sheep pen, the shepherd inspected his sheep for insect bites and injuries;

iv. Guided his sheep patiently to locate food and water and did not drive them like cattle;

v. Watched alertly as his flock grazed;

vi. Rescued his flock (see 1 Samuel 17:34-36 where David rescued sheep from a lion and bear).

It is clear to see why "Lord as Shepherd" was considered a comprehensive metaphor. And, no wonder Jesus refers to Himself as the good shepherd in John 10. No wonder other Old Testament saints referred to the Lord as their shepherd—see for example, Genesis 48:15–16, Isaiah 40:11 and Ezekiel 34:12. Notice, this answers question #1.

b. What do we know about sheep? You might have heard from the pulpit, or even casually in Bible classes that sheep are stupid or weak. Actually, that description is woefully incomplete. Sheep were compassionate, submissive (docile), timid, nervous, and highly social; they did have a tendency to over eat (causing sickness); they were utterly dependent creatures. News flash: we are sheep too; we are utterly dependent on God our shepherd, too (or we should be).

SC[A]R

Analysis begins with asking a few preliminary questions:

- *Who wrote this psalm?* And has this author written other psalms and other works to the Bible? David, the poet, wrote this psalm and many more psalms.

- *Who is the original audience?* As the official hymnbook of the Bible, these songs were used by God's people in Israel; however, this book of hymns were used even in Jesus' time.[12]

---

12. Liderbach, *Christ in Early Christian Hymns*, 42.

- *Why is this book in the Bible?* The book of Psalms or the psalter was the songbook of the people of God in their gathered worship.[13] These songs cover a wide range of human experiences and emotions; so, in many ways, these songs give us permission to express the full range of human emotions from deep mourning to unbridled rejoicing. And while hymns, these songs instruct us theologically and are profitable for training us in righteousness (see 2 Timothy 3:16–17).

- *What is the genre of this literary piece?* We know from Table 2 (Chapter 4) that poetry, such as the psalms, uses heightened or metaphorical language—words and phrases. More about that in a moment.

As music, the psalms indeed have a structure. So analysis reveals this structure for Psalm 23:

[vs. 1] A proclamation of confidence in the Lord;

[vv. 2-3] Notice that each verse begins with "He" (God); here David, a retired shepherd, compares God's care to that of a shepherd caring for his sheep;

[vs. 4] Notice the use of pronouns "I" and "you" and "your"; here David reminds us that in spite of our darkness days, God is with us;

[vs. 5] God as shepherd is replaced with another metaphor, "God as gracious host";

[vs. 6] A proclamation of confidence in the Lord;

Parallelism is a common feature of the psalms, as we see in vv. 1 and 6. It should not, therefore, come as a surprise that this psalm is categorized as a psalm of confidence. We can sense David's confidence in the Lord by noticing where he uses the personal pronoun "I": "I shall not want" (vs. 1); "I will fear no evil," (vs. 4); and "I shall dwell in the house of the Lord forever" (vs. 6).

13. Dennis et al., *ESV*, 939.

Questions and Answers

Analysis continues by examining a few words and phrases in detail, and thus answering some of the questions raised in the "S" step.

Question #4: How do we take "restore my soul"? What is a "soul"? Some believe it is a continuation or result of vs 2—when I experience God's care for me, that revives or restores my soul; others believe, like sheep who go astray and need to be restored, we too go astray and follow after idols, and need to be restored to the sheepfold; and then still others believe that God revives our "going through the motions" type demeanor; when our faith becomes dry, listless, cold, and indifferent—God must at these moments inject us with new vitality.

I think the context argues for all three meanings: a) when I experience God's care for me, that revives me; that excites me; b) I certainly go astray like the 'prodigal son' so it's comforting to know that He will restore me to His sheepfold. Now that's grace; that's mercy; and c) and for me, living the Christian life can become ho hum, routine, mundane, rote, and joyless—I can become like a corpse; so I often need a "pick me up"—I need reviving. Thank God, that He can revive our hearts of stone to hearts of flesh; hearts that beat in step with His heartbeat or hearts that long or pant for Him.

Question #5: "Paths of righteousness"—where are these "paths"? God our Shepherd provides care for us by leading us along "right paths" or "paths of righteousness" for His name sake. God guards His reputation. Because God's reputation is on the line, because His reputation is at stake, He leads us along paths that are right and good for us. Sometimes these paths help us to grow in righteousness. Sometimes these paths help us to rely more on Him. Sometimes these paths God takes us down serve providentially, as "life's little interruptions." God took me down the path of kidney surgery in 2005 and this certainly served as an interruption.

Questions #10 and 13: Metaphorically, what does it mean for God to prepare a table before me? And what does it mean for "goodness and mercy to follow me"?

Question #12: What does it mean for my cup to overflow? This simply means God will abundantly provide us with more than enough so that our 'cups overflow.'

I answered questions #1, #2, #5 and #12 by consulting a Bible dictionary and/or a Bible Commentary. *Notice, I have left questions #10 and #13 for you to answer!*

SCA[R]

Upon arrival to "R"—the Redemptive Remedy, we should also be able to confidently answer these two overarching questions:

1. What aspect of the human condition is revealed in this passage?

2. What is God's gracious remedy for *this* human condition?

What aspect of the human condition is revealed in this passage? The need to be reassured of God's care.

What is God's gracious remedy for *this* human condition? God, as our Shepherd and Dinner host, communicates His unfailing commitment to us; thus, we can be confident of His care.

Meaning of this Passage of Scripture: At the Intersection of Two Answers

The meaning of this beloved psalm can be found at the intersection of the answers to these two questions: What aspect of the human condition is revealed in this passage? And what is God's gracious remedy for *this* human condition? There are moments to be sure when we will doubt God's care; yet we can be confident in God's uninterrupted care and concern.

7

Pulling it All Together:
Applying *SCAR* to
New Testament Passages

THIS CHAPTER APPLIES *SCAR* to *two* New Testament passages: James 2:1–13 and Luke 19:1–10. The book of James fits in the genre of an epistle while the passage in the gospel according to Luke fits the genre of a narrative.

HP#1 reminds us that "The Holy Spirit is our chief superintendent when doing biblical interpretation" . . . so, I offer this brief prayer: "Lord, Holy Spirit, open wide our eyes that we might behold wonderful things from your Word."

SCAR James 2:1–13

[S]CAR

Read James 2:1–13. I invite you to generate a list of questions. Here's my list of questions:

1. When James writes "my brothers" in 2:1, does he mean "my brothers and sisters"?

2. What does it mean to "show partiality"? (vs. 1)

3. James refers to Jesus Christ as the "Lord of glory" in vs. 1—is this significant?

4. Is this a hypothetical or real story/illustration involving a poor man and a rich man? (vv. 2-4)

5. What does it mean to 'become judge with evil thoughts'? (vs. 4). How does this correspond to Matthew 7:1ff where Jesus says "do not judge"?

6. What does it mean "to be rich in faith" and "heirs of the kingdom"? (vs. 5)

7. Does God love the poor only and not the rich?

8. Asking the finely dressed man to sit while instructing the shabby clothed man to stand, is this what James means by "dishonoring the poor man"? (vs. 6)

9. What does it mean to say that "the rich oppress"? Why do the rich drag the poor into court? How do we take "drag"—literally or figuratively? (vs. 6)

10. What 'honorable name' have we been called and what does it mean to 'blaspheme'? (vs. 7)

11. What is the "royal law"? And is "according to the Scripture" significant? (vs. 8)

12. Showing partiality convicts one by the law as a transgressor—what is a transgressor? (vs. 9)

13. What does it mean be "accountable to all of it (the law)"? (vv. 10-11)

14. What is the "law of liberty"? And what does it mean to be "judged under the law of liberty"? Is the "law of liberty" the same as the royal law (vs. 8)? (vs. 12)

15. When does the judgment spoken of in vs. 13 occur? What does mercy mean? How does one show "no mercy"? (vs. 13)

S[C]AR

Literary context analysis

The verses that precede James 2:1–13 and those that come after inform us of a few facts:

1. Apparently, relations between the poor and rich were a real concern among these Christians—see James 1:9–11 and James 5:1–6.

2. James 2:1–13 serves as another illustration of what it means to "be a doer of the word" (see also James 1:19–27). For instance, visiting orphans and widows in their affliction not only serve as billboards of true religion but it also serves as an illustration of being doers of the word (see James 1:27).

3. Those who are impartial demonstrate they are guided by wisdom from above (see James 3:17). Our literary context analysis reaches beyond the confines of the book of James to Galatians 2:6 and the Old Testament where we find similar teaching on not showing partiality. For example, see Deuteronomy 10:17–19 and Leviticus 19:15. In other words, this injunction not to show partiality was given before by God to His chosen people in the Old Testament.

Self-Contained Passage

Our literary context analysis also informs us that James 2:1–13 is self-contained passage of Scripture—we know this a self-contained passage of Scripture because it is about two classes of people: the poor and the rich and one's treatment of both. In this passage, James applies many of the ideas introduced in James 1:19–27 to a specific situation: the oppression of the poor while giving preferential treatment to the rich.

Cultural-Historical Analysis

Our cultural-historical context analysis considers life in this ancient society. Among the things we consider here are geography, modes of travel, rituals, customs, societal structure, dress, architecture, agriculture, family structure, and climate. We also ask about what was happening economically, militarily, politically, religiously, and philosophically. We need resources at this juncture so reaching for resources at this point, like a Bible commentary and/or Study Bible, is allowed.

- *Geographically,* these Jewish Christians were away from Jerusalem—thus the phrase, "to the twelve tribes in the Dispersion" (James 1:1). Specifically, James' readers are dispersed and "are probably to be found in the regions just outside Palestine along the coastline to the north, in Syria and perhaps southern Asia Minor."[1]

- *Socially,* our research highlights a few germane facts:

    - The economic conditions in the Near East in the middle of the first century also corresponded to their locale. Familiar figures in this area were merchants who ranged far and wide in search of profits (4:13–17) and wealthy, often absentee, landlords who exploited an increasingly large and impoverished labor force (5:1–6).[2]

    - A person's class or status in society was communicated by his or her attire. So fine clothing and jewelry was associated with the rich, and shabby clothing was associated with one who was poor.

    - The readers of this letter were predominantly poor materially. As a consequence, they were susceptible to being taken advantage of by wealthy landlords (5:4-6) and of being dragged into court by the rich (2:6) who dishonored their name and the Christian faith. This

---

1. Moo, *The Letter of James,* 49.
2. Ibid.

explains James' admonition to his beleaguered brothers and sisters in Christ to be patient and to remember that their Lord, the judge and deliverer, is at hand (5:7-11).

– And, like the church today, James also addressed the values of the world that had crept into their church context and most importantly into their worldview and practice. One way worldly values had been incarnated in this church was their deference to the rich and their contempt of the poor (2:1-13).

SC[A]R

Our analysis continues with answering a few preliminary questions:

- *Who is the author and has he written other Biblical books?* There are four individuals named James in the New Testament: James the son of Zebedee (see Mark 1:19); James the son of Alphaeus also known as "James the less" (see Mark 15:40); James the father of Judas (see Luke 6:16) and James, the Lord's brother (see Galatians 1:19). Because of the author's familiarity with the Old Testament Scripture and times, James "the Lord's brother"—who later attained a position of prominence in the Jerusalem church (see Acts 12:17; 15:13; 21:18; Galatians 2:9)—is regarded as the author. This epistle is the only work attributed to James in the Holy Bible.

- *Who is the original audience and why was this epistle written?* This book was written for Jewish Christians. We know this because of the many allusions, images, and references to Old Testament people, places, and things. For example, in James 2:21-26 the apostle discusses the patriarch Abraham; there are many references to the "law" in this epistle; and also note the mentioning of Job (5:11) as an exemplar of steadfastness and the prophet Elijah (5:17). The recipients of this letter had been stirred by social discontent and political aggressiveness, as is demonstrated by the repeated warnings against combativeness, malicious speaking, a treacherous state of mind, etc. So, James writes this letter to admonish humility, patience, and loyalty.[3]

- *Why is this book in the Bible?* This book shows those displaced from home how to practically live out our faith. One of the chief areas this book points out is how to manage our tongues.

- *What is the genre of this piece of literature?* The book of James is a written correspondence—whether personal or official; the formal name is an epistle. And why is that important to know? Because discovering the meaning follows its genre.

James: Illustrator Extraordinaire

A careful reading of this letter will prove that James makes excellent verbal illustrations. For example, James uses a horse's bit and a ship rudder in Chapter 3 to describe the power of the tongue (James 3:3–4). These word pictures help us *to hear* the passage of Scripture and enable us to *see* the passage of Scripture. He uses two marginalized groups—then and now—widows and orphans to illustrate the true essence of the Christian religion (James 1:26–27). Likewise in our passage of Scripture, he uses two illustrations and both are introduced with the word "for": vv. 2-4 and vv. 10–11. James concludes this hypothetical story of the rich man and poor man with a rhetorical question (vs. 4): "have you not then made distinctions among yourselves and become judges with evil thoughts?" Those who discriminate or show partiality have not only exalted themselves to the role of judge, but he or she has judged using worldly standards; thus, James can say that these Jewish Christians have become *judges with evil thoughts*. James will imply, later, that to discriminate against the "the other" is a violation of the Old Testament command in Leviticus 19:18 and Jesus' command "to love your neighbor as yourself"—the heart or core of the "royal law."

3. Reicke, *The Epistles of James*, 6.

The "for" in vv. 10–11 introduces James, final illustration. By conveying, here, the unity of the law, James is emphasizing the equal weightiness or seriousness of breaking any law. That is, to commit adultery is considered the same as breaking the whole law; to commit murder is to be law-breaker or transgressor of the whole law; and to play favorites is to break the whole law.

Questions and Answers

Several words and phrases in our passage of Scripture demand a closer examination. I have discovered several questions about words and phrases during the "S" or sit stage. For instance, we asked:

- *Question #2:* What does it mean to "show partiality"? (vs. 1) To show favoritism or deference.

- *Question #3:* James refers to Jesus Christ as the "Lord of glory" in vs. 1—is this significant? Take "Lord of Glory" as a title; a title appropriate here considering Jewish Christians were paying too much glory or homage to human beings.

- *Question #6:* What does it mean "to be rich in faith" and "heirs of the kingdom"? (vs. 5). While viewed as poor in the world's eyes, to be "rich in faith" means when one considers his new status in God's kingdom, he is rich (which echoes 1:9-11). And not only this, but those considered poor by the world's standards await a rich inheritance—the kingdom that God has promised in the future.

- *Question #9:* What does it mean to say that "the rich oppress"? Why do the rich drag the poor into court? How do we take "drag"—literally or figuratively? (vs. 6). The very ones who are hauling (dragging) the poor into court for the sole purpose of exploiting them for an economic advantage are the very ones these poor Christians are heaping favoritism on.

- *Question #10:* What 'honorable name' have we been called and what does it mean to 'blaspheme'? (vs. 7). Not only were these Christians being exploited economically but they were being verbally slandered for their association with Christ as Christians.

- *Question #11:* What is the 'royal law'? And is "according to the Scripture" significant? The 'royal law' is the whole body of commandments and exhortations that govern citizens of God's kingdom; a kingdom inaugurated by King Jesus.[4]

- *Question #14:* What does it mean to be "judged under the law of liberty"? (vs. 12). In his final appeal in vv. 12–13, James commands the Jewish Christians (and including ourselves) to "so speak and so act" according to the law of liberty—the perfect law that gives us freedom—the law that is not burdensome, but rather the law is a grace gift from God that sets us free to serve Him. And all will stand before Him at the judgment to answer either obedience or disobedience to it.

Eschatology

Eschatology is the study of the end times and the events of the end times. The book of James is replete with eschatological overtones. For instance, we find such overtones in James 1:10–11; 3:1; 5:1–11; and find eschatological overtones in our passage with the mentioning of the word "judgment" (2:12–13). James summarizes his teaching, on warning us not to discriminate against anyone, by speaking of the final judgment when God, the Judge, sits on His throne. Essentially, we are told that if we do not show mercy to the poor, then we cannot expect mercy when we stand before God. And the opposite is true: if we show mercy to the poor, we can expect mercy shown to us; thus, God's mercy will triumph over His judgment. Incidentally, we find this teaching of showing mercy to others in Deuteronomy 4:31; Micah 6:8; and Zechariah 7:9. And, James likely heard Jesus say, "Blessed are the merciful, for they will be shown mercy" (Matthew 5:7) and "in the same way as you judge

---

4. Moo, *The Letter of James*, 126–27.

others, you will be judged and with the measure you use, it will be measured to you" (Matthew 7:2).[5]

SCA[R]

Upon arrival to "R"—the Redemptive Remedy, we should also be able to confidently answer these two overarching questions:

1. What aspect of the human condition is revealed in this passage?

2. What is God's gracious remedy for *this* human condition?

What aspect of the human condition is revealed in this passage? It is our human tendency to *play favorites*. In this passage, James commands the Jewish Christians scattered along the coastline to the north, in Syria and perhaps southern Asia Minor, not to adopt worldly or evil thoughts and the concomitant behavior of showing favoritism. To discriminate against others—the poor, those of different race, gender, or sexual orientation—is to break the law: "love your neighbor as yourself."

What is God's gracious remedy for *this* human condition? God's supply or corrective to this human tendency is His Scripture, which is not burdensome, but gives us freedom to act and speak in accordance to His will.

Meaning of this Passage of Scripture:
At the Intersection of Two Answers

The meaning of this passage of Scripture can be found at the intersection of the answers to these two questions: What aspect of the human condition is revealed in this passage? And what is God's gracious remedy for *this* human condition? We are not to

---

5. It is apparent after reading James that he was influenced by and had inculcated much of Jesus' teaching. In fact, Davids argues that "no other letter of the NT has as many references to the teaching of Jesus per page as this one does." New Bible Commentary, 1354.

discriminate against our neighbor—to do so is a sin; we are to rely on the law, God's grace gift, that not only reveals the character of God, but it gives us freedom to show mercy to our neighbor regardless of his station in life, regardless of his race, ethnicity, sexual orientation, etc. Quite simply, I am to be a merciful neighbor to all!

SCAR Luke 19:1–10

HP#1 reminds us that "The Holy Spirit is our chief superintendent when doing biblical interpretation" . . . so, I offer this brief prayer: "Lord, Holy Spirit, open wide our eyes that we might behold wonderful things from your Word."

[S]CAR

Read Luke 19:1–10 and I invite you to generate a list of questions. Here's my list of questions (and some answers and commentary are in brackets "{}"):

1. Where is Jericho?

2. What does the name Zacchaeus mean and does it add any significance to the story? {I ask this question because Biblical names were quite significant markers of a person's mission or fate.}

3. What did a tax collector do? Who was he employed by?

4. How tall was a sycamore tree? Was it a "sycamore tree"?

5. There is no formal introduction between Jesus and Zacchaeus; yet, Jesus calls him by name. What does that prove?

6. "Small in stature"—does that mean Zacchaeus was a midget/ dwarf?

7. Zacchaeus was a "chief tax collector"; how is this title different and the same as a 'tax collector'? Are there other uses of "chief tax collector" in the NT? {This title is only used here in Luke; and this story only appears in this gospel.}

8. How did Zacchaeus get rich?

9. Was it customary for a rich person like Zacchaeus to climb a tree? {It seems a little undignified.}

10. Why did Jesus refer to Himself in the third person as the "Son of Man"?

11. Jesus tells Zacchaeus, "hurry and come down for I must *stay* at your house today"—that seems to convey urgency and divine intentionality—does it?

12. What significance (if any) was associated with having meals together? When did Jesus and Zacchaeus actually share a meal together—before or after—vs. 7? {According to Marshall, Jesus staying at Zacchaeus' home and sharing a meal with him is a sign of fellowship and ultimately, forgiveness.[6]}

13. The crowd grumbled, "He has gone in to be the guest of a man who is a sinner." Why were tax collectors considered sinners? And what does this vocal grumbling say about the crowd's opinion of Zacchaeus and others like him in this profession?

14. Zacchaeus resolves to make restitution four-fold. What did the law require for restitution in cases of fraud? Was this an indication that Zacchaeus radically changed?

15. There is verbal statement that Zacchaeus puts his faith in Jesus—so what's up with Jesus' statement, "Today salvation has come to this house, since he is also a son of Abraham?"

16. What does it mean to be a "son of Abraham"? Was Zacchaeus a son of Abraham by natural or spiritual heredity? {In Romans 4, we are sons and daughters of Abraham by spiritual heredity.}

17. Does "salvation has come to this house" mean everyone in Zacchaeus' home is now saved?

18. What did Zacchaeus' "goods" include (vs. 8)?

---

6. Marshall, *The Gospel of Luke*, 697.

19. Jesus (the Son of Man) came to seek and to save the lost. What does 'seeking' look like? {This "seeking" is the image of shepherd seeking a lost sheep. See Ezekiel 34:4, 16.}

20. What does "save" mean in this context?

21. Who were in the "crowd"? His disciples? Pharisees? Locals of Jericho?

S[C]AR

Literary context analysis

The literary context informs us that Luke 19:1–10[7] is one of several in a series of lessons on money,[8] either directly or indirectly, and its proper use:

- Luke 18:9–14 is a parable about the Pharisee and Tax Collector

- Luke 18:18–34 is about the Rich Young Ruler (RYR)

- Luke 19:1–10 is about another tax collector, who is rich, and how he makes restitution and

- Finally, there is a parable on money in Luke 19:11–27

Moreover, Luke 5:32 and Luke 19:10 form an *inclusio* (statements or actions which serve to interpret the whole which lies between them).

Self-Contained Passage

Luke 19:1–10 is a self-contained passage. Here are the reasons: 1) if we compare Luke 18:35 to Luke 19:1 we see progression: Jesus moves from "drawing near to Jericho" in Luke 18:35 to "He entered Jericho" [*geography/setting*] in Luke 19:1; 2) the two principal

---

7. This account only appears here in the Gospel of Luke.

8. Of all the gospels, Luke says more about money: 11 times in Luke, 3 times in Matthew, and 2 times in Mark.

characters are Jesus and Zacchaeus; but there is also a "crowd" (vs. 3) [and presumably Jesus' disciples were in the crowd?]; 3) there is *coherence*[9]—all the sentences deal with one main idea: Jesus' grace reaches to the lowest of lowest; and 4) Luke 19:10 acts a *summary* statement[10] for the passage and also of Jesus' ministry.

Cultural-Historical Context

Our cultural-historical context analysis considers life in this ancient society. Among the things we consider here are geography, modes of travel, rituals, customs, societal structure, dress, architecture, agriculture, family structure, and climate. We also ask about what was happening economically, militarily, politically, religiously, and philosophically. We need resources at this juncture so reaching for resources at this point, like a Bible commentary and/or Study Bible, is allowed. Note that some of our questions are answered below (see Question # in "{}" below).

1. *Geographically*, this is the same Jericho where Rahab (the prostitute) once lived, but, of course, it was much different at this point in history. Herod the Great had acquired Jericho from the Roman Emperor, Caesar Augustus. Herod proceeded to build aqueducts, a fortress, a monumental winter palace, and a hippodrome. Jericho was one of only three major cities where taxes were collected.[11] {See Question #1}

2. *Socially*, tax collectors were not regarded favorably; on the contrary Jewish tax collectors were considered sell outs or traitors as they were in cahoots with the oppressive Roman government. Tax collectors were ostracized from the Jewish community.

3. *Economically*, the occupation of tax collection was riddled with corruption; a tax collector often charged over and above

9. Doriani, *Getting the Message*, 208.

10 Ibid., 210.

11. Bock, *Baker Exegetical Commentary*, 311.

what was actually required. Zaccheaus was likely the head of the local taxation department. He had others actually collecting the taxes and after settling their accounts with the Roman authorities, he and others would pocket the excess. There was little to no accountability. And because this "system of multiple [tax] collectors, each of whom could add his own surcharge, could create great abuse."[12] Tax collectors got rich by defrauding others. And because they were rich, wore expensive clothing. {See Question #3}

4. *Religiously*, tax collectors were considered sinners and thus ceremonially unclean (Luke 7:33-35). {See Question #13}

5. *Custom wise*, to dine with someone in Jesus' day carried great significance. Hospitality[13] communicated acceptance, fellowship, love, and intimacy. Jesus was not invited to Zacchaeus' home by Zacchaeus; rather, Jesus invited Himself to Zacchaeus' home.

SC[A]R

Our analysis continues with answering a few preliminary questions:

- *Who is the author and has he written other books in the Bible?* The author, and historian, is Luke. He also wrote Acts; in fact, Luke-Acts is considered a two volume work.

- *Who was the original audience?* A crowd that presumably did not believe that the Kingdom of God, which brought salvation, should be extended to the likes of Zacchaeus. See Luke 19:6 for their reaction when Jesus invites Himself to Zacchaeus' home.

- *Why was this book in the Bible?* Luke, a Gentile, gives us the purpose for writing his gospel (see Chapter 1:1-4). A unique feature of Luke's gospel is giving a voice to those on

---

12. Ibid.

13. Hospitality means to "love a stranger" in Greek.

the margin of society or "outsiders" (women, tax collectors, shepherds, prostitutes, etc.). As an example, Luke includes the incarnation of Jesus from Mary's angle. Luke's concern for "outsiders" or "social outcasts" may be attributed to him being a Gentile too. Finally, we get an answer to the question: "Can the rich be saved?" The answer is Yes!

- *What is the genre of this piece of literature?* Narrative. Because there are other gospels, we want to apply the HP#8 *Scripture interprets Scripture* by asking, "is this account in the other gospel accounts?" You will discover that this account is only in Luke.

Narrative Analysis

Since we are dealing with narrative, we once again employ Figure 11. Additionally, because there is talking between the two chief characters, we must also pay attention to words spoken (see Discourse Analysis next).

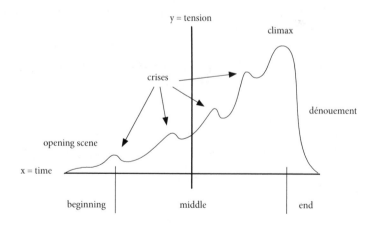

- *Setting/Scene*: Jesus is on His way to Jerusalem for His passion and on His way, He travels through Jericho.

- *Conflict*: Because of his occupation, the crowd essentially keeps Zacchaeus from seeing Jesus so he runs ahead and climbs a sycamore tree. This seems to imply more than a casual interest on the part of Zacchaeus because, after all, as a rich man he was likely in very fine clothes.

- *Climax*: Jesus sees Zacchaeus perched in the tree and summons him to come down; and notice that Jesus says, "I must stay at your home today." Jesus invites Himself to Zacchaeus' home! The grumbling crowd displays their 'collective heart' by expressing their displeasure with the company Jesus keeps: "He has gone to be the dinner guest of man who is a sinner." This tells us about the reputation Zacchaeus and others in his line of work.

- *Denouement/Finale*: What appears to be exasperation, Zacchaeus' "Behold, Lord, the half my goods I give to the poor. And if I have defrauded anyone of anything, I restore it fourfold" (vs. 8), really conveys a remorseful and repentant heart. Was this statement a way of vindicating himself against the accusation that he was a sinner? Jesus answers that question in vs. 9, "Today salvation has come to this house, since he also is a son of Abraham." Jesus, with these words, announces that Zacchaeus' act of making a restitution, which is quite generous, is indicative of a saved man. Jesus' concluding statement in vs. 10 summarizes His mission.

Discourse Analysis and Questions and Answers (See Question# in "{}" below)

Notice in vs. 5 that as soon as Jesus spotted finely dressed Zacchaeus in the tree, He says to him, "Zacchaeus, hurry and come down, for I must stay at your house today." With this statement to Zacchaeus, Jesus demonstrated His omniscience {see Question #5}. He knew Zacchaeus' name without a formal introduction. There is no verbal response from Zacchaeus but he hurriedly comes down.

And like in Luke 15:1-2 when the Pharisees grumbled because of the company Jesus keeps, we get the same reaction here from the crowd after Jesus invites Himself to this chief tax collector's home, a home probably built using funds extorted from his own countrymen (vs. 7), "they all grumbled, He has gone in to be the guest of a man who is a sinner."

Right on the heels of the crowd's voiced displeasure, we hear Zacchaeus' rejoinder in vs. 8, "Behold, Lord, the half of my goods I give to the poor. And if I have defrauded anyone of anything, I restore it fourfold." Zacchaeus' encounter with Jesus radically changed him as this statement reveals a remorseful and repentant heart. Zacchaeus' view of possession was radically changed. Zacchaeus went well beyond what was required by the law to make restitution. According to Numbers 5:5-10, if an Israelite defrauded a fellow Israelite, he made restitution by restoring the neighbor's property plus a fifth or 20 percent. Zacchaeus restored four-fold; thus, after making restitution there is no indication that Zacchaeus had anything left over.[14] {See Question #14}

Jesus makes an announcement directly to Zacchaeus (and indirectly to the grumbling crowd): "today salvation has come to this house." Or Jesus announces that Zacchaeus was saved. And by his actions, Zacchaeus reveals that he is indeed a true son of Abraham (see Galatians 3:7). {See Question #15}

SCA[R]

Luke's gospel is regarded as the "universal gospel" because we find Jesus engaging with people that were on the margins of society: women, lepers, and even Zacchaeus. Yet, we share something in common with the grumbling crowd in this passage: there are some lost people we think are not worthy of being saved. This is a call to repentance and a re-adjustment to see sinners as Christ does: even those like Zacchaeus are worthy of grace, which means we must give sinners our attention and time. Seeking sinners will earn us

14. Tannehill, *Luke*, 124.

criticism as Jesus was criticized. However, Jesus forgets His reputation[15] and associates with a "sinner"—in fact, he lodges at a sinner's house and eats a meal with a sinner. Jesus shows that He is God (namely, His omniscience) by calling Zacchaeus by name without a formal introduction. Jesus is wonderfully winsome toward Zacchaeus. We are called to pick up Jesus' mission and actively seek the lost.

Meaning of this Passage of Scripture: At the Intersection of Two Answers

The meaning of this short narrative can be found at the intersection of the answers to these two questions: What aspect of the human condition is revealed in this passage? And what is God's gracious remedy for *this* human condition? We, like the crowd, in this passage believe that some people are not worthy of God's grace. And so, God's gracious remedy is to remind us in Jesus' interaction with this known crook, Zacchaeus, that just like we were not beyond the reach of His grace, no one else is either.

15. John Piper in his book, "Seeing and Savoring Jesus Christ" says, "Jesus sacrificed His good name to sit with sinners and save them."

8

Conclusion

It is my sincere hope that I have de-mystified the Biblical interpretative task for you with the Hermeneutical Principles (HPs) and introduction and application of *SCAR*. The Bible is, on one hand, a complex book; however, on the other hand, the Bible is a means of grace. Our *Holy God* wants to communicate with us through His Word so that we can know Him better! And God has gifted us with His Holy Spirit and books like this to lend us a helping hand in understanding His Word.

Recall three things: one, an expectation of Biblical interpretation and study—expect to know God more deeply. Packer tells us why, "God's purpose in revelation is to make friends with us."[1] Two, recall from Chapter 1, *Hermeneutical Principles*, one of my favorite quotes, "The revelation of an infinite God by its nature must be complex, multifaceted and challenging to the human mind,"[2] and three, recall HP#10: Hermeneutics is a means to an end; that end is responding to God with all the faith, love, worship, and obedience that He intends.

In light of this expectation, quote, and HP#10, it is my hope that this book will awaken your curiosity and create in you insatiable desire to want to dive into Biblical interpretation. There are so many treasures that await you: knowing God deeply and intimately and growing in the grace and knowledge of our Lord and Savior Jesus Christ (2 Peter 3:18). I can promise you one more thing—knowing God deeply and intimately and growing in the

1. Packer, *God Has Spoken*, 50.
2. Veith, *Why God's Word is All We Need*, 36.

grace and knowledge of our Lord and Savior Jesus Christ will take your worship and obedience of Him to an entirely different level!

So have at it—plentiful treasures and delights await you!

Appendix A: Illustration of Scripture Interpreting Scripture

1. Read John 4:1–26.

2. Look up the verses listed in succession and carefully observe (and hear):

   a. Read Acts 2:38. Notice the *gift of God* in John 4:10 and *gift of the Holy Spirit* in Acts 2:38.

   b. Read Acts 8:18-20. Observe that *the Spirit was given* (vs. 18); Simon wanted the ability to *give the Holy Spirit* (vs. 19) and Peter responds, "May your money perish with you, because you thought you could buy the *gift of God* with money!" (vs. 20)

   c. Read Acts 10:45. Again, we see and hear *the gift of the Holy Spirit.*

   d. Read Jeremiah 2:13, 17:13. God's people have forsaken God, *the spring of living water.* Read John 4:10 again.

   e. Read John 7:37-39. Jesus says those who believe in Him will have "rivers of living water flowing within" and Jesus goes on to tell us that this living water is the Spirit.

3. Conclusion: Based on this evidence, we can conclude that the *gift of God* in John 4:10 is the *gift of the Holy Spirit* that God will give each person who believes in Him.

Appendix B: List of Questions After Reading the Book of Ruth, Chapters 2–4

You will notice that this particular list of questions is more than just questions; it includes my personal notes and preliminary research findings—many of which are documented in the footnotes.

Chapter 2

- Narrator provides some information for the reader (vs. 1); see also 4:1

- "She happened to come to the part of the field . . . "—chance or providence? (vs. 3)

- Boaz proves that he is a worthy man (vs. 1):

    - *encourages* her to glean in his fields and to keep close to his young women (are these female servants or wives?— vs. 8)

    - *charges* the young men not to touch her (vs. 9)

    - *invites* her to get a drink when thirsty (vs. 9)

    - *shows* her hospitality (vs. 14)

    - *demonstrates* generosity with the harvest (vv. 15-16); "do not rebuke her"—was there a limit on how much one could collect?

- What does it mean for Ruth to "fall on her face"? (vs. 10)

- Ruth's story has been told to Boaz; "left your father and mother" is reminiscent of marriage vows (vs. 11)

- Boaz praises and blesses Ruth; what is the meaning of "the Lord repay you for what you have done . . . under whose wings you have come to take refuge"? (vs. 12)

- Being assaulted was a real possibility (see vs. 22)

- How long are the 'barley and wheat harvests'? (vs. 23)

Chapter 3

- Naomi addresses Ruth as "my daughter"—common?; what is meant by "seek rest for you" (vs. 1)

- What is meant by winnowing barley at the threshing floor? (vs. 1)

- Naomi's plan—Ruth to get perfumed up, wait until Boaz is good and drunk and lay at his feet after uncovering them—what exactly is this communicating? Was Naomi's plan conventional or unconventional? (vv. 3–5)

- Does "heart was merry" = drunk? (vs. 6)

- Ruth carries out the 'uncover Boaz' feet' plan. He wakes at midnight and startled to find Ruth at his feet. She identifies herself and request that Boaz "spread his wings over her" (vs. 9)

- Ruth identifies Boaz as a "redeemer"—what are the implications of this title? (vs. 9)

- Boaz continues to address Ruth as "my daughter"—common? Boaz commends Ruth for not going after someone younger than he and promises to settle the matter. And he reiterates what the word on the street is by the local townspeople, "you are a worthy woman." Yet, there is a "redeemer nearer than I" declares Boaz who apparently has the first right to buy or refuse (vs. 13).

Chapter 4

- Was the gate a place to handle business? What is the need for 10 men of the elders? (vs. 1)

- Boaz is crafty in his approach to the next of kin (vv. 3–5)

- What is meant by the redeemer who is nearer to Elimelech's words, "lest I impair my own inheritance"? (vs. 6)

- Narrator explains the practice of confirming a transaction (vv. 7–8); see also 2:1

- "Bought from the hand of Naomi all that belonged to Elimelech and all that belonged to Chilion and Mahlon" (vs. 9)— means what?

- Do we take "bought to be my wife" literally? (vs. 10)

- What practice or custom is referred to by the statement, "to perpetuate the name of the dead in his inheritance"? (vs. 10)—is this similar to Onan's responsibility to his dead brother, Er in Genesis 38?

- What do we know about Rachel and Leah? Perez? And Tamar? (vv. 11–12)

- How will Boaz be renowned in Bethlehem (vs. 11)? Or is this a reference to his offspring?

- The Lord is the Lord of the womb—see vs. 13

- How will this "redeemer" be renowned in Israel? Is the baby meant here or someone else? (vs. 14)

- How is this "redeemer" to be a "restorer of life and a nourisher" of Naomi's old age? (vs. 15)

- Was it normal that "women of the neighborhood" would give a baby a name? (vs. 17)

- Narrator relates the genealogy of David—who was born in Bethlehem; Boaz and Ruth are the great grandparents of King David (vv. 18–22)

Appendix C: Word Studies

How do we choose a word to study?

Verbs describe action so they are often good candidates to study. However, how do we choose which verb to study further? Sometimes the verb will emerge. For example, consider the latter portion of Isaiah 55:2. When we read this verse in the English Standard Version (ESV) and the New International Version (NIV) we find a different rendering:

> ESV: "*Listen diligently* to me, and eat what is good, and delight yourselves in rich food."

> NIV: "*Listen, listen* to me, and eat what is good and your soul will delight in the richest of fare."

Each version of this verse begins with a verb; however, the ESV committee members translated this Hebrew verb as "listen diligently"; while the NIV committee members translated this same Hebrew verb as "listen, listen." I think this is a worthy candidate to study in more detail. Similarly, the ESV translates 1 John 2:2 this way, "He is the *propitiation* for our sins, and not for ours only but also for the sins of the whole world" while *The Message* translates the same verse as, "when He served as a *sacrifice* for our sins, he solved the sin problem for good—not only ours, but the whole world's." Propitiation and sacrifice are both in the predicate position, but clearly they are different words. This difference prompts a word study.

A word like "love" in the New Testament warrants a word study because there were four Greek words in use for the word love: agape, phileo, eros, and storge. The evangelist John uses both agape and phileo in John 21:15–19. Sometimes the mere frequency of a word is a hint that a word is calling out to be studied: "call" and its cognates appear (8) eight times in 1 Corinthians 7:17-24. Likewise, the phrase "sons of the prophets" appear frequently in 1 and 2 Kings (see 1 Kings 20:35; 2 Kings 2:15; 4:1; 4:38; 5:22; 6:1). So, this phrase warrants a closer look. Conversely, the rare mentioning of a word may warrant doing a word study, like 'chief tax collector' in Luke 19:1. In fact, this is the only place in the entire New Testament that this word is used. Understanding the phrase "kingdom of God" (or "kingdom of heaven") is tantamount to understanding Jesus' pronouncement in Mark 1:14–15, so it certainly qualifies as a nominee for a word study. Sometimes, the Holy Spirit will take your childlike curiosity into overdrive, and words will pop off the page as worthy word-study candidates.

Sometimes a word is vitally important to understanding the passage. For example, consider the word "firstborn" in Colossians 1:15–20 (NASB):

> 15 He is the image of the invisible God, the firstborn of all creation. 16 For by Him all things were created, *both* in the heavens and on earth, visible and invisible, whether thrones or dominions or rulers or authorities—all things have been created through Him and for Him. 17 He is before all things, and in Him all things hold together. 18 He is also head of the body, the church; and He is the beginning, the firstborn from the dead, so that He Himself will come to have first place in everything. 19 For it was the *Father's* good pleasure for all the fullness to dwell in Him, 20 and through Him to reconcile all things to Himself, having made peace through the blood of His cross; through Him, *I say*, whether things on earth or things in heaven.

The word "firstborn" is a word that warrants our consideration, because most of the instances of "firstborn" appear in the Old Testament. Let's take a closer look.

How is word study done?

1. Remember Hermeneutical Principle #8: Scripture interprets Scripture. First, consult a concordance, and look up the Scriptures where we find "firstborn." Several Scriptures are listed in *The NIV Exhaustive Concordance*, like Genesis 4:4; 38:7; Exodus 4:22; 11:5; Leviticus 27:26; Numbers 1:20; 8:17; Deuteronomy 12:6; Joshua 6:26; 1 Chronicles 5:1; Micah 6:7; Luke 2:7 and Revelation 1:5.

2. *Preliminary findings.* Most of these verses define the word "firstborn" genealogically; for example,

   a. Abel brought the fat portions from some of the *firstborn* of his flock (Genesis 4:4). Similarly, refer to Deuteronomy 12:6.

   b. Er, was the *firstborn* son to Judah (Genesis 38:7). Similarly, see Numbers 1:20, 1 Chronicles 5:1, Micah 6:7, and Luke 2:7.

   c. God promises that every *firstborn* son born in Egypt will die (Exodus 11:5). Compare to Joshua 6:26.

   d. God declares that every *firstborn* animal – whether to an ox or sheep belongs to Him (Leviticus 27:26). Even every *firstborn* male born to man belongs to the Lord (Numbers 8:17).

3. *Exodus 4:22 and Revelation 1:5.* Notice, I did not comment on Exodus 4:22 and Revelation 1:5 as they are the exception. Exodus 4:22 reads "Then you shall say to Pharaoh, 'Thus says the LORD, "Israel is My son, My firstborn"; and Revelation 1:5 reads "and from Jesus Christ, the faithful witness, the *firstborn of the dead*, and the ruler of the kings of the earth. To Him who loves us and released us from our sins by His blood."

   a. *In Exodus 4:22*, God proudly declares that Israel is His firstborn and Jesus is the True Israelite; so I have a "hunch" that this verse might prove helpful. *Remember it is just a hunch!*

    b. *"Firstborn of the dead,"* from Revelation 1:5, is nearly identical with "firstborn from the dead" in Colossians 1:18 . . . so this might be a true instance where Scripture interprets Scripture.

4. *Consult a commentary on Revelation.* Author Morris says this about Revelation 1:5, "He [John] goes on to speak of Jesus as the firstborn from the dead and the ruler of kings of the earth (compare to Ps. 89:29). Jesus is a figure of majesty."[1]

5. *Consult a Bible Dictionary.* According to *The New International Dictionary of the Bible*, the firstborn son, among the Israelites, possessed special privileges. The firstborn son succeeded his father as the head of the house, and "received as his share of the inheritance a double portion. Israel was the Lord's firstborn son (Exodus 4:22), and was entitled to special privileges as compared to the other peoples. Jesus Christ is described as the firstborn (Romans 8:29; Colossians 1:15; Hebrew 1:6), an application of the term that may be traced back to Psalm 89:27, where the Messiah is referred to as the firstborn of God."[2] This last sentence is interesting: "where the Messiah is referred to as the firstborn of God." In Psalm 89:27 (NAS) we find these words: "I also shall make him My firstborn, The highest of the kings of the earth." *The Message Bible* (a dynamic equivalent) translates Psalm 89:27 this way, "Yes, I'm setting him apart as the First of the royal line, High King over all of earth's kings."

6. *Our conclusion.* Based on Revelation 1:5 and *The Message Bible* rendering of Psalm 89:27, Paul's use of "firstborn" in Colossians 1:15-20 is more than a mere title, or reference to Jesus' birth order as the firstborn over all creation, and the firstborn from the dead. For the Apostle Paul, Jesus stands supreme or as the preeminent one. This explains why the

1. Morris, *Revelation*, 49.

2. Douglas and Tenney, *Dictionary of the Bible*, 353–54.

NIV has this title over the literary unit beginning with Colossians 1:15, "The Supremacy of Christ" or the ESV has this title, "The Preeminence of Christ."

A Word about Word Studies

The good news is that not every word needs to be studied in detail like "firstborn" in Colossians 1:15-20. However, some words must be studied, in detail, as they, like "firstborn," in this Colossians passage, unlock the meaning to the text. Yet, we must be strategic and discerning, as no one has all day to wrestle with word studies! Listening for the Holy Spirit's prompting, and practice, will sharpen your discernment when deciding which words to study.

Appendix D: Making an Investment

Biblical hermeneutics requires research. Research requires consulting with reputable resources. An exegete must (and should) invest in a few resources for his or her home library. Minimally, these resources should include: a Bible Dictionary, a concordance, and an assortment of Bible translations (dynamic and formal equivalents). I have provided here some recommendations for dictionaries, concordances, and Bibles.

Bible Dictionaries

1. J. D. Douglas and Merrill C. Tenney (Eds.). *The New International Dictionary of the Bible* (Pictorial Edition). Grand Rapids, MI: Zondervan, 1994.

2. T. Longman, Ed. *The Baker Illustrated Bible Dictionary*. Grand Rapids, MI: Baker Publishing, 2013.

3. I. Howard Marshall (Ed.), A. R. Millard (Ed.) et al. *New Bible Dictionary*. Downers Grove, IL: Inter-Varsity Press, 1996.

Commentaries

1. Tyndale Old Testament Commentaries. Downers Grove, IL: Inter-Varsity Press.

2. Tyndale New Testament Commentaries. Downers Grove, IL: Inter-Varsity Press.

3. *New Bible Commentary*: 21st Century Edition. Downers Grove: IL: Inter-Varsity Press, 1994.

4. *Bible Speaks Today* Commentaries. Downers Grove, IL: Inter-Varsity Press.

5. John H. Walton, Victor H. Matthews, Mark W. Chavalas. *The IVP Bible Background Commentary: Old Testament*. Downers Grove, IL: Inter-Varsity Press, 2000.

6. Craig S. Keener. *The IVP Bible Background Commentary: New Testament*. Downers Grove, IL: Inter-Varsity Press, 2014.

Concordances

1. James Strong. *The New Strong's Expanded Exhaustive Concordance of the Bible*. Nashville, TN: Thomas Nelson, 2010.

2. Edward W. Goodrick & John R. Kohlenberger, III. *The NIV Exhaustive Concordance*. Grand Rapids, MI: Zondervan, 2004.

3. Also see www.esvbible.org.

Bibles

I prefer (and highly suggest) the English Standard Version (ESV), New American Standard, and Revised Standard Version as my "go-to" formal equivalents; and for the dynamic equivalents, *The Message* and the New International Version (NIV) are excellent choices.

Other Resources

Some other resources worth your consideration include:

1. Denis Bally. *Basic Biblical Geography*. Philadelphia, PA: Fortress. 1987.

2. Jerram Barrs. *Through His Eyes: God's Perspective on Women in the Bible*. Wheaton, IL: Crossway Books, 2009.

3. Gordon Fee and Douglas Stuart. *How to Read the Bible for All its Worth* (Fourth edition). Grand Rapids, MI: Zondervan, 2014.

4. Gordon Fee and Douglas Stuart. *How to Read the Bible Book by Book*. Grand Rapids, MI: Zondervan, 2002.

5. Arthur W. Klinck and Erich H. Kiehl. *Everyday Life in Bible Times* (Third Edition), St. Louis, MO: Concordia Pub. House, 1995.

6. Ron Moseley. *Hebrew Idioms: The Key to Understanding the Bible*. American Institute for Advanced Biblical Studies, North Little Rock, Arkansas, nd.

7. Steve Nichols. *Welcome to the Story: Reading, Loving, and Living God's Word*. Wheaton, IL: Crossway, 2011.

8. Sally Lloyd Jones. *The Jesus Storybook Bible: Every Story Whispers His Name*. Grand Rapids, MI: Zonderkidz, 2007.

9. W. E. Vines. *Vine's Complete Expository Dictionary of Old and New Testament Words*. Nashville, TN: Thomas Nelson, 1996.

Appendix E: Handy "Cheat Sheet"

Use this handy 'cheat sheet' when *SCAR*-ing a passage of Scripture. Remember the Hermeneutical Principles (HPs):

HP#1   The Holy Spirit is our chief superintendent when doing biblical interpretation.

HP#2   Context is Emperor!

HP#3   Beware of the influence of your traditions.

HP#4   Honor the original meaning of the text.

HP#5   Every word is divinely inspired in the Holy Bible; however, the paragraph and chapter breaks are not divinely inspired.

HP#6   Being familiar with the Bible can actually be *an enemy* of understanding the Bible.

HP#7   *Exercise exegesis*; guard against eisegesis.

HP#8   Scripture interprets Scripture.

HP#9   Interpreting God's Word requires humility.

HP#10 Hermeneutics is a means to an *end* - responding to God with all the faith, love, worship, and obedience that He intends.

SCAR: [S]it, [C]ontext, [A]nalysis, and [R]edemptive Remedy

Sit. Read the text many times; and as you read, interrogate the text. Make a list of questions and ask who? What? Where? Why? How? and When? Prioritize this list as best you can. Make some early pre-judgments. Note: *Don't reach for any resources at this point.*

Context. Consider the literary and cultural-historical contexts. Note: from this point on, consult with Biblical resources (see Appendix D).

- Literary Context—consider the passages that sandwich your passage of Scripture; how does reading what comes *before* and *after* my passage of Scripture clarify the meaning of words, phrases, etc.? Can you follow the author's train of thought? How does the 'wider' context of the entire book, testament or Bible clarify your passage of Scripture? Consider outlining.

- Cultural-historical Context—examining this context transports us back into an ancient society; so we ask what was happening politically, educationally, medically, environmentally, technologically, militarily, familially, religiously, philosophically, agriculturally, occupationally, and economically? What were some of the customs and rituals? How did people dress and communicate?

Analysis. Identify the genre as this will drive your analysis path. We ask basic questions like: who was the author? Did he make other contributions to the Bible? Who was the original audience? Why was this particular piece of literature written? Analysis also means comparing reputable Biblical resources and arriving at conclusions. Answer your questions raised during the *Sitting* step.

Redemptive Remedy. Ask two fundamental questions here: 1) what human misery or sin is highlighted in this passage of Scripture; and 2) what is God's remedy to this human misery or sin? The answer to these two questions reveals the single meaning of the passage. Remember, although a passage of Scripture has a single meaning, it, nonetheless, can have many applications.

Bibliography

Adams, Jay E. *Truth Applied.* Grand Rapids: Ministry Resources Library, 1990.

Agan, Jimmy. Adapted from Dr. Jimmy Agan's notes on *Semantic Genres,* Covenant Theological Seminary, 1997.

American Heritage Dictionary of the English Language. Boston: Houghton Mifflin Harcourt, 2011.

Athanasius, Saint Patriarch of Alexandra. *St. Athanasius on the Psalms.* New York: Morehouse-Gorham Co., [1949].

Beekman, John and John Callow. *Translating the Word of God, with Scripture and Topical Indexes.* Grand Rapids: Zondervan, 1974.

Bobo, Luke B. *Does a Second Century Rabbi's Teaching Methods and Process Elements Align with Malcolm Knowles' Andragogical Framework.* PhD diss., University of Missouri-St. Louis, 2011.

Bock, Daniel. *Baker Exegetical Commentary on the New Testament: Luke,* Volume 1. Grand Rapids: Baker Books, 1994.

Butterfield, Rosaria Champagne. *The Secret Thoughts of an Unlikely Convert: an English Professor's Journey into Christian Faith.* Pittsburgh: Crown & Covenant, 2012.

Carson, D.A. *Exegetical Fallacies.* Grand Rapids: Baker Book, 1984.

————. *The Difficult Doctrine of Love of God.* Wheaton: Crossway Books, 2000.

Chesterton, G. K. *Orthodoxy.* Grand Rapids: Christian Classics Ethereal Library, 2009.

Christian Reformed Church. *Ecumenical Creeds and Reformed Confessions.* Grand Rapids: CRC Publications, 1987.

Collins, John C. *Did Adam and Eve Really Exist?: Who They Were and Why You Should Care.* Wheaton: Crossway, 2011.

Cotter, David. *Genesis.* Collegevill, MN: Order of Saint Benedict, 2003.

Dennis, L.T., et al. *ESV Study Bible.* Wheaton: Crossway, 2008.

Doriani, Daniel. *Getting the Message: A Plan for Interpreting and Applying the Bible.* Phillipsburg: P & R, 1996.

Douglas, J. D., and Merrill C. Tenney. *The International Dictionary of the Bible.* Grand Rapids: Regency Reference Library, Zondervan, 1987.

Ellis, E. Earle. *The New Century Bible Commentary: The Gospel of Luke.* Grand Rapids: Eerdmans, 1974.

Fee, Gordon D. and Douglas K. Stuart. *How to Read the Bible for All Its Worth: A Guide to Understanding the Bible.* Grand Rapids: Zondervan, 1982.

Groshong, Lisa. "Rock 'n' roll Holliday." *University of Missouri Alumni Magazine* 96, (2008) 50.

Howard, Jr., David M. *An Introduction to the Old Testament Historical Books.* Chicago: Moody, 1993.

Jobes, Karen H. *Esther.* Grand Rapids: Zondervan, 1999.

Kaiser, Walter C. and Moises Silva. *An Introduction to Biblical Hermeneutics: The Search for Meaning.* Grand Rapids: Zondervan, 1994.

Keil, Carl Friedrich and Franz Delitzsch. *Biblical Commentary on the Old Testament.* Grand Rapids: Eerdmans, [19-].

Klein, William W., et al. *Introduction to Biblical Interpretation.* Dallas: Word, 1993.

Klinck, Arthur and Erich Kiehl. *Everyday Life in Bible Times.* St. Louis: Concordia, 1995.

Kselman, John S. "Psalm 101: Royal Confession And Divine Oracle." *Journal For The Study Of The Old Testament* 33 (1985): 45–62. *ATLA Religion Database with ATLASerials.*

Kostenberger, Andreas and R. Albert Mohler. *What Happened to Truth?* Wheaton: Crossway, 2005.

Liderbach, Daniel. *Christ in the Early Christian Hymns.* New York: Paulist, 1998.

Mare, W. Harold and Murray J. Harris. *1 & 2 Corinthians.* Grand Rapids: Zondervan, 1995.

Marshall, I. H. *The Gospel of Luke.* Bel Air, CA: Paternoster. 1978.

McGrath, Alister E. *Theology: the Basics.* Malden: Blackwell, 2004.

McCullough, James. *Sense and Spirituality.* Eugene: Cascade, 2015.

Moo, Douglas J. *The Letter of James: An Introduction and Commentary.* Grand Rapids: Eerdmans, 1985.

Morris, Leon. *Revelation.* Grand Rapids, MI: Eerdmans, 1987.

Mueller, Jordan. *ENG 45400 Senior Thesis Class Notes.* Lindenwood University, St. Charles, MO (2014).

Oden, Thomas C. *How Africa Shaped the Christian Mind: Rediscovering the African Seedbed of Western Christianity.* Downers Grove: InterVarsity, 2007.

Packer, J. I. *God Has Spoken.* Downers Grove: InterVarsity, 1979.

Peterson, Eugene. *The Message Bible.* Colorado Springs, CO: NavPress 2003

Piper, John. *Seeing and Savoring Jesus Christ.* Wheaton: Crossway, 2001.

Plantinga, Cornelius. *Not the Way It's Supposed to Be: A Breviary of Sin.* Grand Rapids: Eerdmans, 1995.

Postman, Neil and Weingartner. *Teaching as a Subversive Activity.* New York: Delacorte, 1969.

Rahner, Karl. *Foundations of Christian Faith: An Introduction to the Idea of Christianity.* New York: Seabury, 1978.

Reicke, Bo. *The Epistles of James, Peter, and Jude.* Garden City: Doubleday, 1964.

Robertson, A. T. *Word Pictures in the New Testament*. Nashville: Broadman, 1930.

Smith, Robert. *Doctrine that Dances*. Nashville: B & H Academic, 2008.

———. *Guest Lecturer for the Covenant Theological Seminary J. R. Wilson Preaching Lectures* (2005), np.

Sklar, Jay. *Leviticus: An Introduction and Commentary*. Downers Grove: InterVarsity, 2014.

Tannehill, Robert C. *Luke*. Nashville: Abingdon, 1996.

Tennent, Timothy C. *Invitation to World Missions: A Trinitarian Missiology for the Twenty-first Century*. Grand Rapids, MI: Kregel, 2010.

Veith, Gene Edward. *Why God's Word is All We Need*. Wheaton: Crossway, 2000.

Vinson, Richard B. *Gospel According to Luke*. Macon: Smyth & Heylwys, 2008.

Wenham, Gordon J. *Genesis 1-15*. Waco: Word, 1987.

Williams, Margery. *The Velveteen Rabbit*. New York: Henry Holt and Company, 1999.

Williams, Michael. *Covenant Theology Class Notes*. Covenant Theological Seminary (1999), 4–5.

Young, Richard A. *Intermediate New Testament Greek: A Linguistic and Exegetical Approach*. Nashville: Broadman & Holman, 1994.